# Engaging Communities in Museums

*Engaging Communities in Museums* is designed for museum professionals who are hungry for information about how to design experiences in partnership with their communities. Providing an overview of the many ways that museums around the world have begun to listen more attentively to their audience, the book highlights the importance of listening to community and discusses the idea of relationship-building as an entry point to relevancy.

Drawing on interviews and discussions with museum professionals around the world, as well as tangible, real-world examples, Allison showcases the many ways that museums, both large and small, are actively working with their communities and also provides a roadmap that demonstrates how museum professionals can listen more effectively to their audiences as they craft new experiences. The book also explores the fascinating nexus of community engagement and exhibit and experience development, thus taking museum professionals on a journey of discovery around community responsiveness and attention to audience.

*Engaging Communities in Museums* provides a thorough comparison of development models from disparate venues, making the book a must-read for museum professionals who are looking for purpose and common-sense techniques that can guide their work with the communities that they serve. Students in museum studies courses will also find the text useful as a primer on community engagement in museums.

**David B. Allison** is Onsite Programs Manager at the Denver Museum of Nature & Science and has spent his career in museums working to design and develop engaging experiences for audiences of all ages.

# Engaging Communities in Museums

## Sharing Vision, Creation and Development

**David B. Allison**

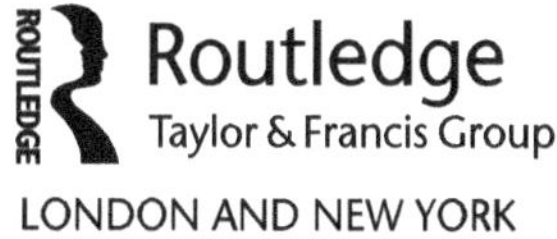


LONDON AND NEW YORK

First published 2020
by Routledge
2 Park Square, Milton Park, Abingdon, Oxon OX14 4RN

and by Routledge
605 Third Avenue, New York, NY 10017

First issued in paperback 2021

*Routledge is an imprint of the Taylor & Francis Group, an informa business*



*British Library Cataloguing-in-Publication Data*
A catalogue record for this book is available from the British Library

*Library of Congress Cataloging-in-Publication Data*
A catalog record for this book has been requested

Typeset in Times New Roman
by Apex CoVantage, LLC

Publisher's Note
The publisher has gone to great lengths to ensure the quality of this reprint but points out that some imperfections in the original copies may be apparent.

ISBN 13: 978-1-03-208678-1 (pbk)
ISBN 13: 978-1-138-48972-1 (hbk)

# Contents

# Acknowledgments

Thank you to my wonderful and passionate co-workers at the Denver Museum of Nature & Science. I am so proud to be part of a team that wants to learn and grow each day. Keep striving to be partners and friends with our entire community!

I so value the museum professionals I had the chance to interview and talk to throughout the course of writing this book. A hearty huzzah to Cassie Chinn, Tine Van Goethem, Franklin Cruz, Cat Jensen, and Jennifer Kramer. Each of you brought thoughtfulness, scholarship, and a strong emotional core to our discussions about community engagement.

Many thanks as well to Heidi Lowther and Katie Wakelin at Routledge for your insightful editorial advice and keen eye toward improving the manuscript.

This is written with love to my family and, as always, my wife Molly.

# Introduction

## Community, museums, and society

It is easy to become troubled and jaded by the emerging signs of societal decay. Worldwide, newly emboldened nationalists promote violence and spew hatred, while inequalities and deeply felt cultural and racial grievances rive us into localized factions. Impending environmental collapse and a growing moral bankruptcy exacerbate our already-fraught politics. Caught in the wake of these movements and pressures, museums can get lost in a morass of competing concerns and demoralized defeatism.

But there is hope. The strength and clarity that emerge from relationships and unity—museums working hand-in-hand with community—places us right where we need to be to positively impact society. The "wicked problems" of today require solutions from everyone, everywhere, working in partnership together. Museums must not exempt themselves from this struggle. Rather, we must redouble our efforts to connect with community and then to use those partnerships to deeply participate in extracting ourselves from the sticky issues that plague our world.

Community engagement is the best way for museums to plunge into the deep ocean of societal distress and to start to make a difference. Co-visioning—finding out what really matters to individuals and community—is the best way to begin relationships of trust between museums and those with whom we wish to partner. Co-creation—working together with individuals and community to design a course of action that springs from a shared vison—is the most effective way for museums to draw from a deep well of creativity and ideas to propel new solutions to effect change. Co-development—the design and implementation of products and programs that provide pathways to enlightenment, learning, and joy—is the technique that draws together community and museums in the harmonious creation of experiences and in problem-solving. This is the challenge and opportunity of museums today.

*****************************************************

## Why co-vision, co-create, and co-develop?

On my commute back home from the Denver Museum of Nature & Science, there is a sharp, curving on-ramp from Colorado Boulevard onto Interstate 70 westbound. I typically take this route, so I rarely think about what is outside the windows as I sit in backed-up rush hour traffic. My mind wanders as I listen to podcasts or news on the radio. Sometimes I groove to music, bopping in my seat to my preferred styles of old-school soul and funk. The end of a day at work is not my preferred time for reflection—my mind is at its most acute first thing in the morning. But on a recent afternoon I had an epiphany as I eased my car into the familiar arcing curve of this ramp.

For the first time in the five or so years that I'd been taking this route, I spotted a pedestrian cutting through the middle of the grassy circle. It is rare to see anyone walking along this section of road, and this man knew exactly where he was going. Without pause, he bounded down the slope from Colorado Boulevard into the middle of the circle. I noticed a well-worn path neatly bisecting the circle and leading to an office park on the other side of the ramp. The designers and builders of the interstate clearly had not planned on creating a walking path. The danger of stumbling on the steep slope, the even greater danger of crossing a ramp in which cars could careen around the curve at speeds as high as 30 miles per hour, and the desire to keep cars and pedestrians as separate as possible resulted in a design bereft of walking paths.

But people are always going to forge a path where none may have been anticipated, because we find the routes we need and then go in that direction, whether or not anyone planned for it. That path through the circle is how our work with communities often ends up. Museums have a plan in mind for what our audiences will be interested in that aligns with our collections or a preexisting story or content point that we want to share. We build our teams and our internal structures so that we can have a clean circle onto the interstate of exhibits, programs, and experiences. Then, when the work is nearly complete or well down the road to coming to life, we share out what we've done with a focus group or a community panel. Perhaps unsurprisingly, our community doesn't want to go to that interstate with us. Instead, they choose to set out across the circle to a different destination entirely.

How can we plan for the path instead of finding ourselves "out of step" with our audience? This book aims to throw a few ideas toward how we can ensure that we don't find ourselves estranged from our community. It's not enough to be responsive—we must be intertwined with and dependent upon the reciprocity and deep participation of everyone with whom we come into contact.

Writing has always been my way to work out cognitive challenges. Fingers to keyboard or pen to paper spools out the daily experiences I have and collates them into stories that make sense. I think about the ink spilled and terabytes of storage and data that have piled up about any topic, and I wonder why anyone would want this addition to the dialogue. But I hold out hope that this will, in fact, hold some use for you. Let's start with the questions you may have.

Why are museums around the world suddenly so interested in connecting with community? Muddled messages from board rooms and the stress of trying to be all things to all people has created a crisis of identity for museums. What role do we play and how do we adapt to a rapidly changing world? A short list of museum "reasons for being" illustrates the quandary that we face.

- Museums are trusted educational resources.
- Museums are bastions of cultural hegemony and patriotism.
- Museums are wonderlands of entertainment and joy.
- Museums are repositories of knowledge and the collected "stuff" of the past.
- Museums are community hubs and gathering places.
- Museums are change agents for building a better society.

How might we wade into this quagmire and emerge on the other side with a purpose? For most museums, we can claim a least a couple of the purposes above. If we're lucky, we have honed in on the ones that best resonate with our audience and have been able to use these purposes to carve out a niche for ourselves in our community.

However, it is clear that large swaths of the 55,000 museums worldwide (31,500 in the United States alone)—have not adequately stated (or even thought through) why they exist.[1] Even today, many museums have mission statements that can be filled in quite easily MAD Lib-style. Invariably, these museums say that they are all about "collecting and preserving ________ to educate the citizens of ________ about ________." If you can complete this fun MAD Lib with your museum's mission, perhaps it is time to reconsider why you do what you do.[2]

In addition, museums have a long legacy to overcome as we seek to connect with underserved and diverse populations. Jason Farago wrote on July 11, 2018, in the *New York Times*,

> A 21st-century universal museum has to unsettle the very labels that the age of imperialism bequeathed to us: nations and races, East and West, art and craft. It's not enough just to call for "decolonization," . . . the whole fiction of cultural purity has to go, too. Any serious museum can only be a museum of our entangled past and present. The game is to not to tear down the walls, but to narrate those entanglements so that a new, global audience recognizes itself within them.[3]

Shucking aside these legacies and crafting new narratives is hard and important work. Moreover, society seems to be spiraling dangerously around us, as newly emboldened nationalists trumpet hate and as increasingly balkanized politics threaten to sever the last remaining strands of cultural civility. But how will another book about museums and community make this any better? What more can be said about a topic that has become wearyingly repetitive to countless museum professionals? The inertia of long days spent in conversations with the people we hope to get ideas from or to court to come to our museums pulls us into quagmires of ennui and empty fields of quasi-philosophical blather about the importance of listening and engagement and relevance. The buzzwords pile up until the cacophony of trite phrases echoes in our ears.

Despite these objections to the topic of community and museums, it is clear that the topic isn't going away in conference sessions, articles and blog posts any time soon. At its core, the desire to engage with "community" revolves around a desire to connect. Sometimes talking about community veers into an othering of groups of people who are not like the traditional white, privileged members of the board and leadership of our organization. Community becomes code for black and brown people or for the elusive millennials who eschew our museums for trendier diversions. We must not let this "othering" become how we think about community. I propose a fuller definition.

When we seek so desperately for universality, we can miss out on the beauty of the quirky stories and culturally relevant experiences that specificity afford. David W. McMillan and David W. Chavis write, "Sense of community is a feeling that members have of belonging, a feeling that members matter to one another and to the group, and a shared faith that members' needs will be met through their commitment to be together."[4]

Clearly, a plurality of Davids are behind this notion of a sense of community. (Does three make a plurality?) For McMillan and Chavis, sense of community is distinguished from the nebulous concept of "community" by feelings. The internal-facing work of building a sense of community cannot be processed and legislated into being. Rather, it must be the hard work of listening and of feeling—being ready to have your heart broken and to break someone's heart. This is the work of the soul rather than of the mind. It also involves action. Note that the "faith that members' needs will be met" can only be nurtured and grow when there are strong relationships of trust that is bound together by a "commitment to be together." Committing to be together even in difficult situations distinguishes a sense of community from work relationships that may grow into community through canny team-building but that start from a transactional, economic, and "professional" place.

What communities do we value most highly? A community is only as valued as the value that it creates. Communities can consist of people who are self-serving. I get together with a group of guys every few months to play euchre and watch movies. We could be labeled a community, but we are certainly not providing value beyond some fun diversion and conversations for the men who gather. Communities elevate and become truly useful when they strengthen and enable those around them and move beyond self-service and into true service and sacrifice.

Humans have always banded together. With the exception of lonely monks cloistered far from civilization and the intentional hermits of far-flung islands, humans prefer to be in the company of other humans. We rely on each other for the smarts and skills we ourselves don't possess. And it's not merely because it is evolutionarily convenient to do so. Rather, it is because we find joy and meaning when we make connections to other people. We get energy and ideas from those who have had different experiences, and we are challenged and pushed to try new things when we are with other people.

The vagaries of the human spirit and psychology mean that within communities, individual members can shape and morph the group to their own perspectives. As we—in our own idiosyncratic way—intersect our lives with someone else, we bring our experiences and skills to the interaction and in the exchange, we both leave richer for having crossed paths.

I am privileged, cisgender, white, and male. Due to structural racism, a long history of chauvinism and the grinding force of generational poverty, I have had opportunities that others have not. Although I am well-intentioned, I can't escape the layers of societal injustices that create the culture and political structure within which I function. And my identities invariably influence how I am perceived by others. I can strive to seem innocuous, non-racist, and as an ally to individuals who are different from me, but I can never fully know what it is like to walk in their shoes or to see with their eyes.

Therefore, I have a responsibility and obligation to empathetically listen. I must subsume myself in their stories and fears. Humility and a recognition that I will always have more to learn and that all people have realms of experience and expertise that I don't have and will never have help me to shrink the footprint I have in this world. More practically, I can also hire and promote people who are different from me so that they can bring nuance and alternative ideas to the table.

I realize at this point that a fuller explanation of both why I am interested in the intersection of community and museums as well as how I have been influenced by projects I have been involved with through my employer, the Denver Museum of Nature & Science (DMNS) will be useful. Throughout this book you will bump up against examples from this museum, so a bit of background context will likely be beneficial for you.

The Denver Museum of Nature & Science's advent in 1900 was as a natural history museum featuring taxidermy specimens staged into dioramas. Expanding over the years to include space science content, prehistoric collections and exhibits, and human health content, and hosting numerous world-class temporary exhibits spanning a range of topics and experiential approaches, DMNS is one of the top museums in the United States.[5] In 2016, the Museum started a new initiative focused on getting people connected to the natural world. As part of the project team, I was excited to really engage with the important work of developing a new experience that would show people why they needed to be in closer communion with nature. Over the course of a year or so of discussions, our team ended up intractably stuck. We thought that we knew what our community needed, but our solutions and ideas were not received with the kind of welcome and enthusiasm that we had anticipated. Instead, after numerous intensive community sessions and after listening intently to our audience, we found that people already felt connected to nature, and so by trying to come up with ways to connect people, we had badly missed the mark. Instead of preordaining what our community needed and then supplying them with it—whether they wanted it or not—we began to ask how we could help our community deepen their connections with nature as a bridge to science concepts and scientific thinking.

DMNS's changed approach to working with our community—based in an acknowledgment that our job was to listen first and then respond—transformed my own perspective on my role as a museum professional. Instead of supplying answers, I needed to ask questions. Instead of creating experiences, I needed to co-create. Instead of developing programs, I needed to develop relationships. Understanding our community's values and motivations became central to our organization's success as well as to my own. This book emerged from my reflections on the trajectory of museums vis-à-vis community and my own experience with the power of true partnership grounded in authentic relationships.

## Museums and community in context

When I was a newly minted homeowner,[6] I attempted to eradicate a mold problem in our tiled shower. I attacked the offending tiles with a rabid alacrity. Swinging my pry-bar like a medieval mace, I crushed and pulled tiles until they mounded around my feet in large, dusty piles. Satisfied that the mold was conquered, I jauntily told my wife that I had fixed the problem and that I'd have the shower back to hosting our dirty bodies in no time.

I quickly discovered that my profound ignorance of even the most basic of home repair techniques rendered my initial bravura into a melancholy realization that I had neither the right tools nor the right expertise to complete the task. My decided lack of handy skills and paucity of the proper tools for tiling meant that the shower stayed unusable until we could hire someone to fix it for us. The shower languished in partially destroyed uselessness as we decamped from our master bathroom to the guest bathroom for our daily ablutions. I learned that if I were to attempt a job of this magnitude in the future, I should be sure that I had the proper equipment and skills to carry it through to the end. The joy of quickly dispatching moldy tiles gave way to the reality of the long, difficult—and pricey—process ahead.

This story allegorically illustrates some of the challenges that come with making connections in the community. It is easier to tear down and destroy than to build and repair. Without the proper tools and expertise for the job, the process can curdle quickly and become untenable. Quick solutions that have not been properly thought through are liable to derail when met with obstacles.

Similarly, working with community to attempt to heal and reconcile with the past is rarely simple. Feeble, half-baked solutions do not result in sustained success. Effective community work requires the right tools deployed at the right time to get the job done. As community leaders and museum workers, our voices matter and can engage with the discourse of our times.[7] Here we will explore not only *why* we must prepare ourselves to engage with our community, but also will explore *how* we might start to do this work.

## Community engagement as an imperative for museums

Understanding museum origins and how museums initially framed themselves in relation to the public is helpful for us as we seek to discover the role of community in museums today. Early European museums were guardians of "Western" culture and as temples to Enlightenment knowledge. With this heritage, many museums still maintain a high culture-low culture dichotomy. In addition, wealthy collectors gathered their artifacts in exclusive galleries meant exclusively for the eyes of other rich people.

Collections set aside for the privileged morphed into what we call museums. These museums became fixtures in European cultural centers and presented a sanitized vision of an orderly world. Eighteenth-century scientists were obsessed with organizing and categorizing the human, plant, and animal inhabitants of the globe and sought to reinforce their belief in the perfectibility of a humanity that could remake the natural world in their image.[8] Natural history museums became the most trademarked reflection of this perspective, as they built large cases and "curated" objects by size, importance, or taxonomic grouping.

Another strand of museum origins traces back to Cabinets of Curiosity and zoos, which initially sought merely to entertain and titillate—a thin vein of specious science and dubious historical artifacts provided a cover for a greedy money-grab. The distance between lowbrow entertainment—circus menageries and hucksters—and highbrow cultural transmission and guardianship—the cavernous, marbled halls of the Louvre—seems wide.[9] However, a closer examination shows that both strands of museums had the same view of their patrons. The people who come to these museums were to be spectators and consumers, not active participants. The public needed to be educated and entertained and

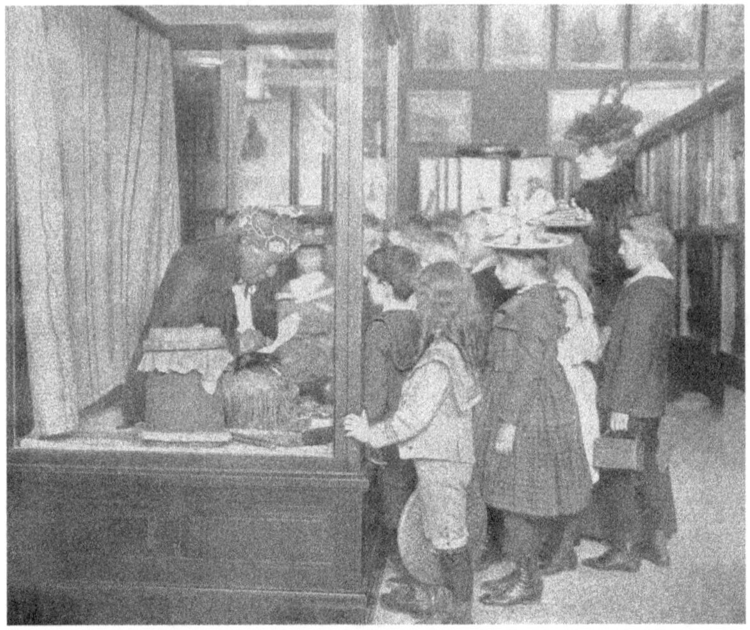

*Figure 0.1* Fourth-grade children view a native behind glass at a museum. This sort of "othering" of native peoples was characteristic of most natural history museums around the turn of the 20th century.

Source: Johnston, F. B., photographer. *At the Museum—Fourth Grade*, 1900. [Photograph] Retrieved from the Library of Congress, www.loc.gov/item/2010 646536/. Photo courtesy of the Library of Congress.

were to be totally beholden to the experts who curated exhibits—or promoted spectacle—for their benefit.

The heritage of these dual strands of museology continues to shape the perception of museums today. Researchers from IMPACTS (Intelligent Models to Predict Actionable Solutions) recently concluded that,

> People don't necessarily feel welcome or that they "fit in" at cultural organizations . . . data shows that, on average, approximately 4 out of 10 people in the US don't feel comfortable at an art, science, or history museum—including science museums and historic sites.[10]

Museums continue to be alienating for much of the public, despite their attempts to break down barriers for their audience.

Significant barriers to museum participation were well entrenched and pervasive until a widespread democratization of museums in the 1970s and 1980s. Learning theory and an increased focus on evaluation showed that participatory education and shared authority were more effective ways to engage the public than didactic, static exhibits and presentations. In addition, museums increasingly sought to understand their role in communities. History museums founded as hagiographic paeans to the "great men" of the past began to tell alternative narratives from the perspectives of the people who worked for the wealthy elites. Natural history museums turned away from trumpeting the ascendancy of white civilization in favor of championing an environmental ethos of shared responsibility for the earth. Art museums sought to showcase lesser-known and minority artists to bring new stories to light.

Since the 1990s, many museums have worked to become integral parts of the day-to-day life of specific localities. These museums are storytellers that connect people to their past, rather than bastions for wealthy collectors to display the trappings of power and prestige. Robert Archibald shares this perspective: "This is not the 'master narrative of old' that defined insiders and outsiders, but instead a process of story-making that creates room for the diverse and multiple perspectives that exist in consequence of our individuality."[11]

Museums are uniquely positioned to open dialogue in their communities. Museums are trusted.[12] Numerous studies have shown that museums are viewed by the public as attractive leisure-time destinations that provide both education and entertainment.[13] Museums are also viewed as mostly impartial and as trustworthy sources of information.[14] These advantages give museums a unique and potentially influential place in society. With this influence, museums can take up the mantle as a trusted convener and as arbiter of difficult issues within a community.

In short, museums must listen to community. Museums that withdraw from the important dialogue of our times risk the slow death of irrelevance. Moreover, community is the barometer against which we can determine our value to the people who keep the doors open through their continued patronage. But how do we know when we are successful in meeting our community where they are and providing for their needs? What are the strategies that propel us toward becoming trusted partners and reliable forums for open dialogue?

## Strategies for working with community

Community is a term that can be so vague as to lose all meaning. It is laden with multifarious definitions, tends to be overused, and is rarely applied consistently. Sheila Watson in *Museums and Their Communities* (2007) attempts to fashion some solid toeholds for the term: "The essential defining factor of a community is the sense of belonging that comes to those who are part of it and that, through association with communities, individuals conceptualize identity."[15] In most contexts, this definition suffices. However, the word "community" can sometimes be used pejoratively, as one group of people define themselves in opposition to another group of people. Also, when museum professionals refer to community, a cynical view would say that they are instantaneously "othering" whomever they are talking about—these are people not like themselves who need to be reached in order to increase attendance, to drum up financial support, or to cultivate as a focus group for new initiatives.

This transactional view results in broken trust and a patronizing sensibility that reasserts the museum's power to exert control over narratives. Rather than cultivating community as "this for that," it must be approached from a place of humility and grace. Indeed, in the words of author Elizabeth Crooke, "Community is both a process and a product."[16] The process—how we approach relationships and build trust—is key to effecting change.

Successful museums will also take on interesting partnerships in order to advance their mission and to build their cache in the community. Relationships built on a shared language of trust and respect can yield important insights as museums seek to design and develop new experiences and programs. An empathetic, conversational approach to sharing authority with our audience is the best starting place.[17]

A number of my colleagues and I at the Denver Museum of Nature & Science were recently prototyping some new offsite programs at Swansea Elementary School in Denver in a fifth-grade classroom. I happened to notice a couple of hand-written signs on the wall of the classroom that speaks to the importance of persistence in relationships. One sign read, "All relationships have bad days. . . . We might not be able to undo the harm that's done." The other sign finished the thought, "but together, we can problem solve and create something stronger and more beautiful."

Developing relationships is difficult. Even the simple act of reaching out to non-traditional museum-goers can be fraught. Diversity can be described as giving someone an invitation to the party. Inclusivity means that once they are at the party, you actually ask them to dance.[18] Efforts to include new voices in museums can be taken as tokenism or as insincere if we do not listen carefully and take proactive action in response to what we hear.

When it is done well, the insights we gain from deep listening can be intensely humbling as we end up in new and uncomfortable places. Must we always preserve our "authority" as experts? What do we uniquely bring to the table when we meet on equal terms with community? Addressing these questions *before* we set out on the difficult journey of relationship-building will set us up for success long into the future.

From Appreciative Inquiry to Stanford design thinking and other for-profit project management models, museums have a range of techniques from which to draw.[19] Which is right for you? The community in which you find yourself should determine what tools to use and how to blend techniques for maximal impact. As has been explained, for most museums, there will not be a single silver bullet that leads to success. Rather, a combination of approaches will yield results. Once a foundation of audience responsiveness and partnership has been built, community work can proceed in a number of intriguing directions.

Working hand-in-hand with community is even more important when addressing seemingly intractable historical situations. Mistrust spawned by years of racism, systemic poverty and neighborhood neglect create adversarial relationships between government officials and citizens. Seismically divergent ways of perceiving the world places wedges between citizens, and bureaucratic gridlock grinds change initiatives into useless dust. When difficulties creep in, how can museums and leaders within communities rise above the fray?

Museum's role as leisure-time options has sometimes resulted in a milquetoast retreat from difficult topics. Thinkwell's 2017 Trend Report included a telling statement that is worth quoting in full:

> [Researchers] heard from patrons that they were coming to museums as a pleasurable escape and were put off by exhibits on challenging, topical content, such as global climate change or controversial historical periods. On the other, they also heard from patrons demanding just that type of content, feeling it's the role of a museum to tackle the "tough topics" like global warming or racism. Museums voiced that they felt stuck, and were unsure if it was a case of "a few loud voices" or if, really, the chasm was widening. The data informed Thinkwell's Trend Report that overall, people are going to these places for fun, entertainment, and to engage together as a family. "Escape" also ranked high. This doesn't mean people don't *also* want a deep and resonant experience, but it does mean that it isn't as strong a driver. Museums shouldn't shy away from tackling the hard stories, but they should keep in mind that visitors are still looking for a pleasurable time.[20]

Museums have the obligation to provide fun, entertaining diversions for the pleasure-seeking public, whilst also opening crucial conversations about the controversial topics of our day. The nuance required to maintain this sort of balance as civic passions are enflamed is substantial.

## When tempers flare and passions rise, how do we mediate effectively?

Some months ago, I found myself at a town hall-style forum about a new development project in Denver. Explosive growth in metro Denver recently has meant that longtime residents—often Latino and low-income—have been marginalized and priced out of their neighborhoods by gentrification. As community members, representatives from city government, and elected officials gathered, the tension and angst became palpable, and it seemed likely that we were in for a long night of vigorous debate.

After a string of polished presentations from city officials, community members began to share their opinions. Ranging from well-reasoned and brief to rambling and interminable, participants' thin strands of patience began to fray as similar-sounding arguments and entrenched perspectives were repeated by person after person. Becoming increasingly churlish, the meeting organizers began to withdraw from the dialogue. This seeming retreat from engagement only served to raise community members' ire and to increase the surly atmosphere in the room.

The gray clouds continued to choke the proceedings, until one city councilperson thanked the community members for being at the meeting and then shared their personal connection to the neighborhood and why they were excited about the project. The icy ill will that had built over the previous hours began to melt away as that individual's positivity shone through. Other community participants who had been silent were freshly emboldened to share their enthusiasm. Both city representatives and community members felt comfortable and ready to share their ideas and concerns from a place of respect. The meeting went from the clogged arteries of rancorous discord to the free-spirited gusto of true dialogue.

Crucial to this flipped situation was the bravery of one individual.[21] In this case, this person was able to make the proceedings less about the problems in the community and more about shared goals and common purpose. Their personal story and good humor elevated everyone and gave new life to the discussion. They found common ground and showed empathy toward community members.

Museum professionals and community leaders must rely on empathy as a tool toward creating a shared understanding of how our communities might embark upon collective engagement with the past. When we perceive and share in the experiences of other people through genuinely seeking to listen to their ideas, needs, and values, we enhance our connectedness to each other.[22] This connectedness, in turn, enables us to see outside of ourselves and to envision a better future.

Ultimately, empathy, compassion, and deep listening are the tools that will allow us to value restorative justice and our shared humanity over narrowly defined self-interests and blindly followed personal peccadilloes.[23] When ignorance of history, reliance on tradition, and power politics intrude upon community engagement, museum professionals and community leaders must band together as trusted conveners to initiate respectful, open dialogue. Finding our shared humanity and common purposes will enable us to be ready not only to address the difficult issues in our community, but to do so with a grace and a willingness to change ourselves as we learn and grow with others.

## How to read this book

*Engaging Communities in Museums* is intended to be a book that you can "drop in on" like you do with a friendly neighbor when you need some advice or need to borrow a tool to finish some yardwork. Rather than reading this straight through from this word to the final period, please find the pieces that you need and leave behind the rest. This book is structured to provide both theoretical as well as practical advice around working with community. Chapter 1, "Community Responsiveness and Understanding Audience," provides a foundation for why partnership and work with community is valuable and necessary. Chapter 2, "Relationship-Building and Partnerships in Museums," shows how museum professionals can start the process of getting to know the people they want to serve through the difficult, yet rewarding, process of forming relationships. Chapter 3, "Case Studies in Co-Creation," shares the stories of museums large, small, and midsized, through interviews with individuals who have been intimately involved in community work. From Canada to Belgium and the United States and Australia, examples of effective community partnership can be found throughout the world. These case studies provide a small glimpse into the hugely varied ways that museums have made strides toward true engagement with community. Chapter 4, "Comparing Models of Development," delves into the methods and techniques that museums and businesses have used to create and develop programs and to build their teams for sustained relevance and utility for their audiences. Chapter 5, "Staying Connected with Community," shares some tangible ways that museums can maintain relationships and continue dialogue beyond the immediacy of a one-off project or program.

Transforming our practice so that we engage in long-range, strategic thinking that gathers all of our resources and relationships to the table will be essential for museums as we seek to expand our reach and influence.

**************************************************

The concept of risk-taking has gained prominence in museum circles recently. Catching on belatedly to trends in the business world, museums are often backwards-looking and laggards when it comes to taking on new ways of doing things. When we talk about risk, we're typically not speaking from the perspective of legal risk—although this is certainly a topic worth exploring—but rather the idea of taking risks that might jeopardize our standing in the community or might end up in a "failed" project that doesn't draw the numbers we anticipated or hew to the high standards or fidelity we desire. We sometimes try to moderate the risk-taking impulse by claiming that we are taking a calculated risk. This modifier gives us peace of mind by implying that we have some metrics or research that back up our risky move. However, the very definition of risk means that when it is done best, we look at the data and past experience and thumb our nose at it as we dive headlong into new ways of viewing the world. How might you begin to view the world differently as you connect with those around you? This is where work with community must start.

## Notes

1. See Ingraham, Christopher. "There Are More Museums in the US Than There Are Starbucks and McDonalds Combined." *Washington Post*, Jun. 13, 2014. www.washingtonpost.com/news/wonk/wp/2014/06/13/there-are-more-museums-in-the-us-than-there-are-starbucks-and-mcdonalds-combined/?utm_term=.c4abbfc60270. Accessed 26 Jun. 2017. Also, https://museumplanner.org includes statistics about worldwide museum numbers. Feb. 26, 2019.
2. Sinek, Simon. *Start with Why: How Great Leaders Inspire Everyone to Action*. London: Penguin Press, 2009.
3. Farago, Jason. "A New Type of Museum for an Age of Migration." *New York Times*. www.nytimes.com/2018/07/11/arts/design/germany-mobile-worlds-mkg-museum.html. Accessed 26 Feb. 2019.

4 McMillan, David W., and David M. Chavis. "Sense of Community: A Definition and Theory." *Journal of Community Psychology,* vol. 14, Jan. 1986.
5 DMNS qualification for a "top museum" can be measured by attendance—2018 saw over 2 million visitors onsite and offsite—as well as respect in the field for high-quality content. DMNS also employs 14 PhD curators.
6 Fun tidbit—the word "meow" is nestled (like a cat curled up in a blanket) within the word ho*meow*ner. If that doesn't give you "paws," what will?
7 Museums are implicitly trusted by the vast majority of the public. See "Public Perceptions of—and Attitudes to—the Purposes of Museums in Society" (A report prepared by BritainThinks for Museums Association, March 2013), 3.
8 Godkin, Edwin Lawrence. "A Word about Museums." *The Nation,* vol. 1, Jul. 27, 1865, pp. 113–114. Godkin's screed against P.T. Barnum's American Museum is fascinating for its fantastically demeaning view of the lower classes. A representative remark in which he mentions that the lower classes will not be able to go to Barnum's museum because it burned down reveals this distain, "The worst and most corrupt classes of our people must seek some new place of resort" (113). Godkin continues by calling for a new "American Museum" in New York City that would hew to the standards of the British Museum and elevate the status of museums in the United States. The "American Museum" Godkin referred to eventually became the American Museum of Natural History (AMNH).
9 See Allison, David. "The Power of Amusement." American Alliance of Museums *Alliance Labs* blog, Oct. 21, 2017. http://labs.aam-us.org/blog/the-power-of-amusement/. Accessed 25 Dec. 2017.
10 Dilenschneider, Colleen. "Cultural Organizations Are Still Not Reaching New Audiences." *Know Your Own Bone.* www.colleendilen.com/2017/11/08/cultural-organizations-still-not-reaching-new-audiences-data/. Accessed 17 Nov. 2017.
11 Archibald, Robert R. *The New Town Square: Museums and Communities in Transition.* Walnut Creek, CA: Alta Mira Press, 2004, p. 14.
12 "Public Perceptions of—and Attitudes to—the Purposes of Museums in Society" (A report prepared by BritainThinks for Museums Association, March 2013), 3.
13 Falk, John H., and Lynn D. Dierking. *Learning from Museums: Visitor Experiences and the Making of Meaning*. Walnut Creek, CA: Alta Mira Press, 2000, p. 28.
14 "Public Perceptions of—and Attitudes to—the Purposes of Museums in Society" (A report prepared by BritainThinks for Museums Association, March 2013), 3.
15 Watson, Sheila, editor. *Museums and Their Communities*. New York: Routledge, 2007, p. 3.

16 Crooke, Elizabeth. *Museums and Community: Issues, Ideas and Challenges*. New York: Routledge, 2007, p. 32.
17 Frisch, Michael. *A Shared Authority: Essays on the Craft and Meaning of Oral and Public History*. Albany: State University of New York Press, 1990, p. 10.
18 Attributed to Denver's Deputy Mayor Allegra "Happy" Haynes.
19 For more information about Appreciative Inquiry, see Whitney, Diane, and Amanda Trosten-Bloom, *The Power of Appreciative Inquiry: A Practical Guide to Positive Change* San Francisco: Berrett-Koehler Publishing (2010) by Diane Whitney and Amanda Trosten-Bloom. For details about Design Thinking, see *Design Thinking: Integrating Innovation, Customer Experience, and Brand Value* (2009) New York: Allworth Press by Thomas Lockwood.
20 Mitchell, Katherine. "Thinkwell's 2017 Guest Experience Trend Report." Nov. 17, 2017. https://thinkwellgroup.com/news/thinkwells-2017-guest-experience-trend-report/. Accessed 25 Nov. 2017.
21 Also important in this situation was food. Community members brought homemade green chile, noodle dishes, and desserts to the meeting. Food brings us together and reminds us that our shared humanity is given beautiful expression in relationships built over the breaking of bread.
22 See Gokcigdem, Elif M., editor. *Fostering Empathy Through Museums*. Lanham, MD: Rowman & Littlefield, 2016. In this book of case studies and essays, Gokcigdem is able to make a compelling case that empathy is business and moral imperative for museums. Empathy is the first step in developing transformational experiences at museums that also have the potential to transform society.
23 Ibid.

# 1 Community responsiveness and understanding audience

Earlier this year, the reality of the difficulty of true partnership struck home for me. My colleagues and I had begun a partnership with a new arts group in town. The Denver Museum of Nature & Science (DMNS) had been successful in working with these sorts of groups for our Scientific and Cultural Facilities District (SCFD) Free Days in the past, so we applied the same processes and systems to this new relationship.[1] We tried to work in the same way that had worked well with our other partners, and it all fell apart quickly, as miscommunications, unmet expectations, and mishaps resulted in hurt feelings and a subpar final product.

This situation made me realize that we can never just claim "we got this" and sit back and rely on systems and processes to bring success. A mechanistic approach that removes the core of relationship from a partnership is constantly at risk of getting thwarted by the sticky gray areas of interpersonal communications. New relationships must be nurtured and carefully cultivated and not left to the whims of impersonal systems. Large organizations are particularly susceptible to bogging down in process and to failing to connect individually with people.

Systems are built upon an accretion of assumptions. Over time, people create ways to get work done without conversations and in ways meant to make work easier or quicker for one group of people. These layers of assumptions become the inflexible systems that are obstacles to effective communication and partnership.

DMNS had done this work before and had been successful. We thought the stubbed-toes days—the bad times when misunderstandings, hurt feelings and thwarted plans were the norm—were far behind us. Relationships are non-linear and cannot be boxed in by systems, so of course in this new situation with new people involved, we found ourselves with new challenges. The human dimension of partnership work results in endless potential outcomes and limitless possibilities. This is the terror and the thrill of true engagement with community.

Looking to the past for guidance in the future is always helpful and rewarding. And please trust me that I'm not just saying this because I love history—contextualizing our work provides us with a stronger foundation upon which to build for the future. In addition, museums have already tested and tried a plethora of techniques and approaches over the years, and listening to the wise sages of the profession and their ivory tower allies can provide succor and strength as we identify our purpose.

Evaluators and the insight they provide into what our audience wants—both qualitative and quantitative—are another huge asset in our hunt for purpose. I once sat around a table with colleagues in a meeting intended to identify strategic initiatives for the future. The question was posed, "What do people want to know about our state?" Then the five of us shared our opinions. "People like skiing around here, right?" "Beer is cool. You know, because of hipsters." "What about food—locavores and eating lower on the food chain?" "We have a great collection of agricultural crap. Maybe an exhibit about the Oliver plow would be good?" "STEAM is all the rage! Art, technology, and entrepreneurship are the wave of the future." It was just five different people with five different opinions about what we should do. Not one of us said, "What would our audience say that they wanted?"

One of my assumptions about museums is that we will never find our purpose if we don't listen carefully to our audience. Another assumption is that in a world of alternative facts and daily assaults on well-established scientific and historic truths, discovering and articulating our purpose is absolutely essential. The last assumption that I bring is that museums should be places of wonder and joy. My experience and philosophical beliefs about museums have led me to the conclusion that museums best serve the public if they start from the viewpoint that they are leisure-time options for people. If we begin there, the other multifarious purposes to which we aspire add a richness and depth to the foundation of fun that we have built.

Museums have often suffered from being late to trends. Moving quickly to capture the zeitgeist does not come easily to us, and we often find ourselves aping other successful experience providers rather than pioneering new ways of delighting our audience. Must we always be playing games of catch-up with the world around us? Pop-up museums have usurped our name and aim to create selfie moments around every corner. What would move museums out of the pale imitation game and into the realm of true experience innovation?

Each of us has our own idiosyncratic approach to life. We contain bundles and worlds of interests and ideas. Likewise, museums offer a wide range of options for our audiences. A quick glance through TripAdvisor or Yelp reviews of museums shows that some guests love interactive, modern, and digital interactives. Others are aghast by those techniques and seek out contemplative, quiet experiences in austere, beautiful settings.

Moreover, psychologists have shown that most humans are remarkably bad at reflective self-assessment. The Dunning-Kruger Effect—named for two researchers at Dartmouth University—posits that people of low ability often overestimate their own capabilities, resulting in overconfidence and misplaced trust in their own intelligence. Moreover, these individuals also do not recognize their own lack of awareness and are unable to adequately reflect on their failings.[2] Because we are so bad at this sort of self-reflection, we often elevate our own opinions and ideas above others and rarely stop to examine our biases.

The Dunning-Kruger Effect also leaves us vulnerable to hubris and can estrange us from other people. These barriers to successful relationship-building can be crippling to museums as we attempt to work with community. In addition, we fail to recognize when our actions and the accretion of our traditions and history are at odds with what the community values. This sort of blindness to community is rampant in museums, and we must do our best to reinstate reflective self-assessment.

This reflection is at its best when we can position ourselves as having a positive social impact through our work. The Oakland Museum of California is one museum that has made this goal explicit. They have a social impact statement defining what they hope to be in the community, "OMCA makes Oakland a more equitable and caring city."[3] The next natural question is to ask how to measure this social impact. Traditionally, visitor demographics as corresponding to the community's demographics (i.e. do we serve a smaller percentage of African-Americans in our total number served than the percentage of the population of African-Americans in our city) has been the primary measure of social impact. Nina Simon suggests that it an "organization should strive to *exceed* [emphasis hers] community demographics for groups that may be marginalized or excluded from other cultural resources."[4] Moreover, she argues that individual impact and the depth and quality of the experience are more valuable measures than a raw increase in numbers served by a museum or the change in demographics over time.

When social impact and community engagement is embraced broadly by the entirety of a museum—from the board of directors and CEO to the front-line staff—we can begin to transform our society. Taking what can be perceived as a "political" stand can be dangerous, but as Mike Murawski writes, "We just need to take bold steps to value the skills, interests, culture, and heritage of our communities and neighborhoods and begin to de-center the traditional power structures of museum institutions."[5]

As we acknowledge and make amends for our past, we must likewise examine ourselves with a view toward a humble reification of our identity and a new commitment to listening and empathy. The journey toward rebirth, both personally and organizationally, will be arduous. Change is difficult as our humanity asserts its self-righteousness and as we refuse to examine our motivations. There can be no true transformation without such work, however. Seeking to find pathways to better understand and serve everyone is the highest goal toward which we can aspire.

## Tools for transformation—understanding audience

At the end of each chapter, I will provide a few applications and practical tips that you can try out at your own organization. For this chapter, I will focus on evaluation and how to gain insight into your audience's needs, motivations, and perception of your museum. For many museums, evaluation may be an afterthought or may seem too difficult to pull off with tight budgets and a paucity of human power. However, investment in evaluation is never wasted. Understanding your audience is essential to crafting experiences that are resonant and relevant.

It is important to start an evaluation program by paying attention to data both quantitative—attendance, demographics, and time and tracking studies—and qualitative—suggestions, expressions of needs, and interviews about perceptions of the organization. These twin strands of evaluation build a network of meaning upon which all museum staff can have a shared understanding of how their work intersects with their community.

Dusty notebooks of post-visit evaluations and summative project reports sitting on office shelves or clogging up email inboxes and hard drives do no one any good. It's time to pull those out and "truth check" your assumptions against the real comments and input of your audience. Evaluation for its own sake is not useful. Rather, we must seek to inculcate a culture of evaluation followed by remediation or action to redress problems and issues that are revealed by the data. Checking our assumptions against actual audience feedback is one of the best ways to ensure that our programs and experiences do not stray from alignment with our community.

Social media and internet review websites provide museums with another tool to evaluate their success. Google, TripAdvisor, Facebook, Yelp, and many other sites provide starred ratings and comments about museums and cultural organizations. While it is true that often the people who comment on these sites are "outliers"—folks who either have an axe to grind based on a perceived slight or who have had a particularly exceptional experience that they want to crow about—it is usually possible to get a fair picture of overall guest perception of your organization from these sites. Moreover, there are services available that will compile internet data and comments for you, making a daily temperature reading of the organization's health possible.

Additionally, one-on-one interviews, focus groups, and community panels are often the best way to get rich, in-depth information about specific museum initiatives and projects. These conversations give nuance and texture to cold, hard quantitative data. Chapter 4 of this book shares a few specific techniques that you can use to get the most useful information out of these conversations. You'll also learn how you might design these encounters so that they build strong, mutually respectful relationships and create lasting connections between your organization and its community.

## Notes

1 The Scientific and Cultural Facilities District (SCFD) is a special tax zone in counties surrounding Denver (and in Denver) that supports cultural organizations in those areas. As a "thank you" to taxpayers, the Denver Museum of Nature & Science offers 12 Free Days and/or Nights for the community. These have developed over the years to be true celebrations that feature face painters, large dinosaur puppets, and other festive performances and activities. They are also great days to bring in partners to share activities. See Chapter 5 for more information about Free Days at the DMNS.

2 Dunning, David. "The Dunning-Kruger Effect: On Being Ignorant of One's Own Ignorance." *Advances in Experimental Social Psychology*, vol. 44, 2011, pp. 247–296. Academic Press.

3 McKinley, Kevin. "What Is Our Museum's Social Impact?" *Medium*, Jul. 17, 2017. https://medium.com/new-faces-new-spaces/what-is-our-museums-social-impact-62525fe88d16. Accessed 12 Dec. 2018.

4 Simon, N. "Are Participant Demographics the Most Useful Single Measure of Community Impact?" *Museum 2.0*, Feb. 20, 2018. http://museumtwo.blogspot.com/2018/02/are-participant-demographics-most.html. Accessed 20 Nov. 2018.

5 Murawski, Michal. "Towards a More Community-Centered Museum, Part 3: Defining & Valuing Community." *Art Museum Teaching*, Oct. 1, 2018. https://artmuseumteaching.com/2018/10/01/towards-a-more-community-centered-museum-part-3-defining-valuing-community/. Accessed Jan. 15, 2019.

## Bibliography

Janes, Robert R. *Museums and the Paradox of Change*. Calgary: University of Alberta Press, 1997.

Weil, Stephen. *Making Museums Matter*. Washington, DC: Smithsonian Books, 2002.

# 2 Relationship-building and partnerships in museums

When I first began working in museums, I was enamored of the potential for conversations with guests to spark curiosity. Person-to-person interaction—whether through facilitated programming, shows, or first-person enactment—is often the most effective way to get people interested and excited in a topic.[1] The unique interplay and exchange of two individuals with different perspectives and life experiences coming together for a brief moment in time to talk with each other and to learn something new can be beautiful to behold. Museums provide these opportunities. When a guest chats with a volunteer or staff member at a museum, it's not the typical interaction with strangers that we experience elsewhere. It's not a transaction at Starbucks, where after a brief exchange of pleasantries, the cashier will expect us to proffer money in exchange for a warm beverage. Instead, it's a moment with no expectations on it other than enjoying some conversation with the goal of understanding something better. Guests can opt in to these conversations—they can attend programs and approach docents, or they can avoid people and read labels and participate in interactive exhibits on their own.

Guests are free from the pressure of transaction and commerce as they explore the many, many entry points and open-endedness of a museum visit. This freedom heightens the obligation we have to make those brief moments with that individual in front of us as rich and meaningful as possible. Moreover, we must use that time to do more than just teach a content point.

For a long time, museums have used Maslow's hierarchy of needs to convey the importance of catering to guests' basic needs before trying to teach them anything. The idea that guests need to have easy access to bathrooms, comfortable chairs to rest, and a plenitude of food options is, by now, a well-worn trope. What if the goal of what we do isn't to teach, but is rather to make connections? What would happen if we see our jobs as not to pour content into empty vessels, but to build onto pre-existing networks of prior knowledge after we've established a friendship with our guests? To take this further, what if instead of seeing the people who come to the museum and who we make contact with out in the community as guests, visitors, patrons, audience, etc., we see them as acquaintances who have the potential to become friends?

Friendships blossom out of meaningful time spent with another person. The moments we have can build on each other over time, so that instead of being mere "interactions" or "touches"—numbers that count toward our yearly total visitation but say nothing about the lasting impact of the headcount—we build up a network of friends and trusted collaborators who are ready to stand alongside us. People who count on us and whom we can count on. In this way, museums distance themselves from businesses that are merely out for profit and show that our value lies in who we are, not in what we have in our collection or in the educational aptitude of our exhibits.

The best feedback I receive about a staff member or volunteer is when a guest says that they really felt listened to and cared about by them. I rarely hear comments about how much someone learned. Rather, the impactful guest experiences are when a staff member takes the time to get to know someone. Then, the comments from guests are about the amazing time they had with an individual and how fun they were, or how interesting they made the content. People only learn when they are comfortable and ready to do so. This happens best when the experience is rooted in relational interactions.

If we can lift people up and feed their souls in the same way that we feed their minds, we will provide a positive service that makes us a haven of encouragement. We should do this, first, because it is the right thing to do, and second, because we will find ourselves more successful as our attendance increases. The next section features an anecdote from early in my museum career that may be disturbing to some readers. Please take this as fair warning. However, my intention in sharing this story is not to shock or titillate, but rather to illustrate an important aspect of our own psychology as it relates to community work at our museums.

*******************************************************

I had never butchered an animal before. A few of the veteran men on staff who had been butchering for many years asked me to come along and help, and I set off with them down the slope through the woods to try to herd the hogs toward the pen at the bottom of the hill. The hogs ran surprisingly fast through the trees, and we had to move quickly to cut them off from escape. It was a gray and chilly November day. The dead and browning leaves crunched under my boots. We had to use rakes and sticks to pat and move the hogs toward the gate to the pen. Once inside, they could tell that something was amiss, and they squealed and scrabbled in dismay and fright. A couple of guys opened a gate on one side and pushed one of the hogs into this separate area. One man had a long, sharp knife at the ready. Another had a .22 rifle and took aim right between the pig's eyes. The rest of us watched from a safe distance. A sharp report issued followed quickly by a squeal and a grunt. Rushing up to the hog, the man with the knife sliced the pig's jugular vein, blood gushing out all around. Two large Percheron horses were at the ready and in harness, pulling a flat cart. Now they asked me to help hoist its still-warm body onto the cart. It took six of us in the end to heft the carcass. The same man who had sliced the pig's neck also made small cuts on its back legs. Then someone else took a wooden hanger and inserted it between the hog's Achilles tendons. This complete, we tied the hog's front legs to the cart and headed up the hill to the yard to the side of one of the historic cabins on the property.

As the hog was strung up on a large frame above a steaming kettle of boiling water, I thought about the brutality of the moment and wondered how I had gotten here. Nothing in my city-dweller experience had prepared me for this, and I was woefully unready to engage in this work. As the morning wore on, we pulled the hair off the hog and then removed its entrails. Next, we cut the fat off the carcass and started to render it down into lard. Beginning to carve out specific cuts of meat, some other staff members had already begun pan-frying the tenderloin for our lunch. As I sat eating the freshest meat I'd ever had, I came to realize that by experiencing butchering this intimately—seeing the hog's death throes and then assisting in processing the dead animal—my respect for the life that the animal gave for me to be nourished had been hugely increased. I would never eat meat again without true, heartfelt thankfulness—a thankfulness informed by my firsthand experience butchering.

I share this story of hog butchering to emphasize the importance of firsthand experience. Nothing motivates change more effectively than deep, personal understanding. I would never have had that epiphany about my consumption of meat if I hadn't had the chance to participate in butchering. Likewise, we must be active participants in the tough work of community-building and partnership development if we want to be changed and influenced by people who are not like us. It is nearly impossible to be transformed by sitting blithely on the sidelines watching the world go by.

One way to get more involved in the day-to-day experience that guests have at our museums is to pay attention to evaluation. Audience data and evaluation should lead museums to becoming more entrenched in their community and better equipped to flex to the needs of their audience. Community responsiveness is about more than mere lip service in the form of panels or community advisory boards—it needs to reflect a community focus in all aspects of museum operations. This sort of deep engagement with community has its genesis in relationships.

Relationships are the pieces of ourselves that we share with others as we build toward common understanding. Shared experiences and dreams become part of the process of relationship building. The ties that form as our own personal needs and desires are subsumed into care and concern for other people create the foundation upon which community and partnership form. This is hard work and not for everyone. Mechanistic or transactional approaches to relationships have no place in a positive, empathetic, community-driven development process.

Successful museums take on interesting partnerships in order to advance their mission and to build their cache in the community. Relationships built on a shared language of trust and respect can yield important insights as museums seek to design and develop new experiences and programs. An empathetic, conversational approach to our work is the best starting place.

Developing relationships is hard work. When it is done well, developing relationships is an intensely humbling endeavor that drags our museums into new and uncomfortable places. Must we always preserve our "authority" as experts? What do we uniquely bring to the table when we meet on equal terms with community? Addressing these questions *before* we set out on the difficult journey of relationship-building will set us up for success long into the future.

The lines of connections to museums are many. Are we attractions? Do we align ourselves with amusement parks and family entertainment centers (FECs)? Certainly these sorts of venues are our competitors for scare leisure-time dollars. Maybe we're more similar to our cousins in libraries? We aim to provide educational opportunities and a gathering place for people to talk about things that matter to their community. What about coffee shops or local bars? Are we places for people to hang out and enjoy their friends and family with mildly diverting collections, exhibits, programs, and art surrounding us?

Perhaps we're none of these. The public sees us as different, and we occupy a space that means something—both good and bad—to people. Museums have a long legacy of colonialism and white privilege to combat. Happily, what we offer to our guests is joy-filled, rich experiences that can enlighten, inspire, and entertain. This helps the pill of our past to go down easily. The past must always be swallowed and is ever-present in how we manifest in the present, but when our present has been stripped of the entangling snares of racism and injustice and embraces a socially engaged core, we find ourselves as trusted conveners and reliably benign entertainment venues. Our educational missions and the hopeful services that we offer underserved communities around access to programming and exhibits that might benefit them put us in a benevolent non-profit category for most people. Places like Denver and St. Louis have even been successful in passing taxes that fund non-profit arts, science, and history organizations.[2]

The difficulty has been in making a case to funders that supporting our missions through financial donations can create the same sort of impact as social service organizations whose mission it is to better the lives of people through providing food, shelter, and other basic needs for humans. Museums are clearly beneficial to the public. People receive a sense of well-being from learning something. They can feel closer to their family and friends through leisure-time activities like museum visits, thus strengthening the social fabric. They can have their curiosity piqued and set their interests into new directions. But these are ethereal, apparitional impacts. They fall well short of the world-changing work of social-sector non-profits.

It is incorrect, however, to downplay the margins in which we play. These margins can take on outsized impact for individual lives and can be inspirations for new ways of seeing the world. Numerous studies have shown that formal education often cannot inspire the same sort of life change that informal cultural organizations and museums can. This research shows that at least in the area of education, museums have a definitively useful societal function—and one that is worth funding and supporting across multiple types of museums and over a wide range of time.

Taking our work too seriously leads us into the trap of self-importance. Museums that can look objectively at themselves and have a laugh and bring their audience in on the joke will be ready to do good, humble work with community. Leadership that approaches their job with less focus on control and on keeping the message tight and close to the vest will be able to liberate their staff to play and innovate with the work of the museum. This playful approach can endear us to the people we serve and will help us to form the lasting partnerships that will drive museums beyond relevance and into the realm of necessity.

## Tools for transformation—partnerships

Finding partners is often less about seeking them out than it is about serendipity. A quick conversation at a gathering, a fortuitous linkage from a colleague, or a wayward email snagged in the ninth hour by an attentive staff person can be the catalyst for partnerships. Starting small with a partnership is a great way to test the waters before diving in with longer-term obligations and programming. At DMNS, we often will bring in new partners for one-day events where we know we'll have a large audience and an infrastructure of staff and spaces ready to support our partner's activities.

Another tip that you can use when developing partnerships is to look outside of your traditional ken. Do you often collaborate with other art museums? Try to find a youth choir instead. Do you feel most comfortable working with people who are your own age? Push yourself to reach across generations. Are you grounded in the reality of scientific evidence and objective facts? Seek out a faith-based organization to challenge you.

Good partnerships will follow their own meandering stream. Instead of setting hard and fast goals, give your partnership time and space to breathe and to find its own footing. Generosity—both toward ideas and with time and resources—breeds the sort of goodwill that draws new and quirky partners to you. Be unfailing generous. Partnerships receive life-giving sustenance from generosity.

## Notes

1 Allison, David B. *Living History: Effective Costumed Interpretation and Enactment at Museums and Historic Sites*. Lanham, MD: Rowman & Littlefield, 2016.

2 Some would argue that these sorts of special tax districts may not be a net benefit—especially for smaller, marginal organizations—as the money from the government ends up artificially buoying poorly run or inefficient organizations that would be driven to extinction or forced to function more efficiently by market forces.

## Key references

Adair, Bill, Benjamin Filene, and Laura Koloski, editors. *Letting Go? Sharing Historical Authority in a User-Generated World.* London: Routledge, 2011.

Falk, John, and Lynn Dierking. *The Museum Experience Revisited.* 2nd ed., Walnut Creek, CA: Left Coast Press, 2012.

Johnson, Anna, et al., editors. *The Museum Educator's Manual: Educator's Share Successful Techniques*. Lanham, MD: Alta Mira Press, 2009.

*Mastering Civic Engagement: A Challenge to Museums*. Washington, DC: American Alliance of Museums, 2002.

# 3 Case studies in co-creation

As we've explored, listening is the first and best step in working with community. This chapter is another form of listening. Here will we stop to glean tips and best practices from successful practitioners. What follows are lightly edited transcripts of conversations or correspondence I had with these individuals. From Brussels to Vancouver to Seattle to Australia, and from an anthropology museum to art museums and science museums, the tools and techniques are as varied as the museums from which they emerge. What you choose to adapt and borrow will be unique to your own circumstances. Glean what you will here and leave behind what will not work in your situation. The end of this chapter has a short summary of lessons we can glean from each of these case studies.

***************************************************

## The Wing Luke Museum

In August 2018, I had the chance to interview Cassie Chinn, the Deputy Executive Director of the Wing Luke Museum in Seattle, Washington. The Wing Luke is primarily a visual arts museum whose collection is focused on Asian art. Chinn began at the Wing Luke in the early 1990s as an intern, and she was instrumental in starting the museum's community-based exhibit development process.

DAVID ALLISON (HEREAFTER REFERRED TO AS DA): Tell me about the Wing Luke Museum's community exhibit development process.

CASSIE CHINN (HEREAFTER REFERRED TO AS CC): Our museum has always been community based. I oversee all programming. I started in the early 1990s as an intern and then was the first exhibit staff. In 1992, we brought community members together to talk about an exhibit about Japanese incarceration during World War II. We directly involved people in the beginning. We worked with the community to create a show to tell stories that hadn't been told before. My job was to formalize the process of creating exhibitions with community members.

We used an exhibition development model, but we integrated community as decision-makers, not just as advisors. Our role at the museum as facilitators is to listen to their vision.

DA: Could you describe how you begin the process of working with community groups on an exhibit?

CC: The first meetings are an opportunity to get to know each other and to determine the scope before diving into content. We have to ask—what is the main message? Then we break into subthemes. We start from a high level to get the framework and then we get more and more concrete.

Next we ask what the storyline is for the show. We use a bubble diagram form, then we add more specifics; such as the look and feel. Honing in on the emotions is the focus. The advisory committee contributes a story-based oral history. It starts with 12 or 15 people once a month. Then as we progress, more people's voices are added. They have a role in reviewing materials and then are involved as we transition to the exhibit opening and public programs installation.

DA: How do you maintain your connection with community and balance their needs with the needs of the organization?

CC: The key is really transparency in communication. We have to stop and take the time to find out what they care about and then we work on it on our end. Then we bring it back to them and work with them through the decision-making process. We sometimes have to ask ourselves what the original intent of an idea was and then recognize that there are multiple ways to achieve that intent.

Through everything, we have to demonstrate that we are listening and not just gatekeepers. It is about trust. We are focused on relationships and on developing long-term relationships with community. Once we have that trust, we have to have accountability. I want our community to be able to call us on things.

DA: What are some of the ways that your community work has changed over time?

CC: Every time we do a project or exhibit, it's a new experience. What are the needs of this particular community? The decision-making is different for each group. We are deeply engaged in finding cross-community connections and in coalition-building. The Asian-Pacific communities are changing and diverse. We are also now asking ourselves, how can this process and our mission reach outside the Asian-Pacific community? We are refocusing this model that we've used now for over 20 years. What new applications for new communities can this have?

## Bozar Centre for Fine Arts

In July 2018 I spoke via Skype with Tine Van Goethem from the Audience Engagement Department at the Bozar Centre for Fine Arts in Brussels, Belgium.

DA: Tell me a little about the exhibit you put on last year in 2017.

TINE VAN GOETHEM (HEREAFTER REFERRED TO AS TVG): The *Yo!* exhibit was about hip-hop. It was primarily intended to be political, not artistic. We tried to focus on the neighborhoods and students for our audience engagement.[1]

DA: How did you work with community to develop this exhibit?

TVG: We were funded in large part by the BRUSSELS CAPITAL REGION. Time was a big issue for our partners (Visit Brussels, Centre Bruxellois d'Action Interculturelle) at the Brussels Centre for Intercultural Action. Bozar engaged volunteers to work together on the creation of the interactive space in the exhibition, workshops with artists from Brussels, classes for children ages 6 through 18 in the city with local partners. Then on Fridays, the students and parents would come to Bozar to dance, enjoy the music, and to show their parents the exhibition. The goal was to bring them from the neighborhoods to the museum. The exhibit had an interactive and performance space, as well as a studio to perform.

DA: What was successful for you in your work with community?

TVG: We set out criteria early on. We wanted to build relationships. We quickly found out the importance of contacts—it was really not just calling people, but having a real dialogue on equal grounds! We engaged a student to do follow-ups and contact people afterward. With limited human resources it was hard to do thorough evaluation.

We realized we needed to create a win-win and to develop a new exhibition and a range of workshops—beatbox, rap wars, hip-hop dance, graffiti, DJing and rap as well as other classes organized by partners. We also needed lots of departments working together. The low cost for participants—1 euro versus 45 euro normally—was necessary to provide access, was a strong communication tool. The one euro being equal to one access was possible thanks to grants.

DA: Tell me how Bozar intends to continue this work?

TVG: We know that there are structural difficulties to this work. We want people to visit our organizations and to build sustainable relationships. We have to ask ourselves—what are the right channels to enable humans to talk to other humans? We also dealt with some criticism of the content of the exhibitions. And we also had an institutional timeline for people who didn't want to be institutionalized. Artists were not as engaged as could have been. The will to work with community is not only about the money, it's about making choices (and the difficulty of the choices). It is so important for museums to invest in social projects. And it's important to continue the dialogue and sustainable relations with the communities, which also means that the institution has to invest in human capital to continue.

## Franklin Cruz, Denver Museum of Nature & Science educator/performer, social activist, and performance artist

On November 13, 2018, I spoke with Franklin Cruz, an educator/performer at the Denver Museum of Nature & Science. His perspective on museums and community as a front-line staff member is shaped by his life experiences and is highly useful as an avenue to view museums and museum workers through the lens of social activism.

DA: Tell me more about professionalism. How do you see that concept getting in the way of effective work with community groups?

FRANKLIN CRUZ (HEREAFTER REFERRED TO AS FC): Due to professionalism, we often create barriers or stigmas that interfere with our communities. Many times in our effort for inclusion and diversity we reach out to groups outside of our cultural and profession norms without addressing, acknowledging or ascertaining how we may disrupt theses norms to make people feel less stigmatized and othered because of norms we subconsciously promote in our policies and attitudes.

Professionalism is really a class-oriented norm that has been drawn out of a typical business model. This model is based on white standards and capitalism. Capitalism has a reductionary approach to time in which money and time are equated and it forces people into Eurocentric standards of time. Malleability with time makes us more humanistic and focuses us on other people and on operating relationally.

Think about how attire denotes ingenuity and capacity for many people—what is this person wearing and what do we think about them based on their comportment? Because these ideas about professionalism are so tied in with Eurocentrism, it is important to question why we continue to value professionalism so highly.

DA: Tell me more about your concept of intersectionality as it applies to museum work.

FC: As an example I like to use concepts from biology and ecosystems. People don't often see the connections between a mountainous ecosystem and the oceanic ecosystem. Really it is water that is the connector between the mountains and the oceans. The rain falls in the mountains and then whatever is in the mountains ends up in the ocean. They impact each other through water. It's not dirt or wind, but the water. And you can see this with butterflies as well. When there is a problem—like the fires in California that produces smoke that ends up in Colorado and then impacts Monarch butterfly migration to Mexico—we can realize that this interconnectedness creates and interplay between one another.

All this to say, we must examine how our intersections are meeting in museums. How people of color with different abilities are able to move through the building and how they are treated, as we can see from the example of the mountains. How families with non-English-dominant households and different nationalities feel entering a space with no displays in their language equates to the ocean. Then we can begin the true work of how these audiences are received and considered in our planning, communications, projects, and the theory we weave into our operations daily—which corresponds with the water from the example above.

DA: What role does the history of the United States have in how museums in this country deal with issues of power and privilege?

FC: I think that Americans are short-sighted and unaccountable for their history. We need to take accountability for where we come from. My Chicano heritage includes colonizers along with indigenous peoples and I need to take responsibility and own those roots. I still hold those systems of oppression and erasure within me and just acknowledging that is a first step.

We have to each look at our background and heritage and look back at what we should give up from the past. It's like when you have a rich friend who gives you all sorts of amazing helicopter rides and nice things, but you realize that they have been ruining your relationships with all your other friends and actually make you even more unhappy than you were before. It's time to give up that relationship. Break up with your privilege.

DA: What should museums do or not do in the coming years?

FC: Whew. That's a loaded question. Start with returning collections. Appropriation needs to stop and museums should say, "These were stolen" whenever they display artifacts that were stolen. Just naming it is important. Here at the Denver Museum of Nature & Science we can say, "We killed all these animals and we now know that what we did was wrong." It's important to not even say the word "but." Let's stop excusing it and own it.

I think translation into other languages is really important as well. Museums talk about the budget and difficulty of translating, but to be welcoming we just need to do it. What about having iPads with Google Translate on it for all languages? Language is so powerful and provides the welcome that is needed. Making the effort is so important.

Also, think about the concept of professionalism and how to measure impact differently. Professionalism looks at numbers, but qualitative evaluation can get a better depth of feedback on what we're doing and its success.

Combining art, science, and nature is key. I start all my talks with a poem. Instead of abstracts on papers, we should include poems. Art makes things affordable and provides access in new ways to people who would otherwise just get bored.

## Cat Jensen

Immediately following is a brief sketch of Cat Jensen's career highlights—this overview is useful as a backdrop for the dialogue which follows. In this exchange, Jensen gives a highly personal—and exceedingly applicable—recounting of her relationship to identity and museums.

Cat Jensen has loved museums since the time they got lost in a dinosaur exhibit when they were five. For nearly a decade, they have worked in history, science and anthropology museums (San Diego Museum of Man, Denver Museum of Nature & Science, and Four Mile Historic Park, among others) as an actor, teacher, guest services specialist, historic interpreter, program coordinator, gallery manager and curriculum creator. They have a BA in Anthropology and a BA in Innovation: Women's and Ethnic Studies from the University of Colorado, Colorado Springs and an MA in Cultural Sustainability with an emphasis in Identity Studies from Goucher College. A trained workshop facilitator, their work centers around creating public space intentional about social justice and transformation. When not ghost hunting and wearing many other hats for several historic house museums, they consult with communities across the country for Story+Structure, a human experience design firm dedicated to creating a more compassionate and inclusive planet.

DAVID ALLISON (HEREAFTER REFERRED TO AS DA): Can you explore your work in museums as it relates to identity (yours and others)?

CAT JENSEN (HEREAFTER REFERRED TO AS CJ): Yes! I think identity is at the forefront of all work. Who we are has an incredible impact on how we show up in space, what we bring with us and how we will engage or are able to engage with what is there. I love the concept of third space where Michael Hickey says,

> "Third space" isn't home, and isn't work—it's more like the living room of society at large. . . . It's a place at least one step removed from the structures of work and home, more random, and yet familiar enough to breed a sense of identity and connection. It's a place of both possibility and comfort, where the unexpected and the mundane transcend and mingle.

Inspired by this, when I go into a museum or public space, I ask myself, *is this somewhere I would come back and hang out? Is this a place where I can find peace from the things that bring me sorrow, explore a human experience more deeply or take action for a cause I care about?*

While I always see myself represented everywhere as a white person, I don't always as a non-binary, queer, femme, and someone living in chronic pain with additional ability needs that aren't visible. When I see visibly queer folks of any additional identity in a museum, my heart flutters and I feel instantly more comfortable. Pronoun pins in public space have made me cry for feeling seen. When there are places to sit and take in an exhibit and give my aching body rest, I am more likely to stay longer and leave the experience feeling connected, not just for practical reasons, but because it communicates to me that someone thought places to sit are valuable, for folks of so many needs and identities. I witness others also finding relief and peace in taking a rest and it becomes a way to connect and pause with one another.

I was fortunate enough to visit the Swedish History Museum in Stockholm a couple years ago where in partnership with the Unstraight Museum, they had a project called Hidden Histories. They asked members of the LGBTQ+ community to insert themselves into a narrative they had been historically excluded from. As a guest in the space, I read excerpts next to works of art, statues, and even panels about battles, speaking from a range of LGBTQ+ experiences and identities. Bringing a modern perspective to events that happened over a hundred years ago, as well as folks saying, "as a person of [this identity] I see myself in this historic work but not this one . . ." was reaffirming and made the exhibit come alive in a new way.

It was also the first time I saw some of my own identities represented in a format that wasn't just an entire exhibit about a community within the context of a single time period or event, but a way to say, *look at how people have always existed and continue to exist and should be leading this conversation*. LGBTQ+ identities weren't being rendered invisible or assumed to have never existed, or being presented by someone outside of the community, as marginalized identities typically are.

This is what museums should do and have a responsibility to do. As a cultural worker in this profession and someone with a lot of privilege, I have a responsibility to reflect on experiences like these, harness empathy with identities not my own and take action to critically challenge what stories are being told and by whom in the organizations I work with, including myself.

Representation is not a fad or a phase or a buzzword. It can be enough to determine if someone will spend five minutes and never think of your space again or come back so regularly you get to know them. It can determine whether or not someone feels safe enough to make it in the door.

An essential part of identity is also about the history of the space itself. Museums have long been complicit in historic and social racism, colonization, and identity erasure. We should be asking, *what indigenous community's land is your museum on? How did the building of it contribute to their forcible removal? If not present during the removal what cultural resources did the researchers, scientists, archeologists, and anthropologists at your museum acquire without consent? How is information presented? Who has and is making those decisions and does that need updating? How is the organization working holistically and across all departments to address historic truths, take ownership for them, and do better?* These are the things that keep me up at night.

Luckily, there are already a great amount of resources on this for museums specifically and many places putting them into practice. I owe a lot to museums I've worked for where leadership and fellow educators are working to answer these questions. When working at an anthropology museum where decolonization is becoming a part of everyday practice, I was asked to define terms like, "decolonization" and "institutional racism" in my interview. Required reading for staff included, *Decolonizing Museums* by Amy Lonetree and *Decolonizing the Mind* by Ngũgĩ wa Thiong'o. I am so grateful for that. The learning wasn't only focused on content, but how we get there and deliver it with an understanding of ourselves and our histories. I now include a land acknowledgment in all email signatures and am writing information about these practices into training manuals.

Even little things have an impact. Your museum or historic site or garden or outdoor education center doesn't have to declare decolonization or anti-racism or ability or gender identity and expression inclusion a focus of curriculum or an exhibit to do this work: it's the way you greet everyone when they come in the door, notify folks of anything they might need throughout their visit, ask a learning group of any kind if they have any multi-language or ability needs before they get to your space, the font next to a painting being in a legible and good sized font.

Museums are also spaces of great learning, fun, joy and positive impact. They provide people space to escape what does not bring them joy and engage in something they might not on a daily basis (I get to see how astronauts freaking eat in space!? I can hold that piece of history!? You want to hear how much I know about this artist and geek out about it with me!?) and also challenge societal norms and expectations and I love them for it.

Museums as third space makes so much sense to me! I am always trying to ask myself, *what am I doing right now that is opening space for joy? Is this program igniting curiosity? How much can I learn from as many guests as possible in the next 20 minutes? What about this program brings me joy? If it isn't or doesn't what can I do to change my relationship to it? I have to share with someone how incredible that guest interaction just was or how cool that group of learners were!* These are the things that keep me going throughout the day. And the coffee in the break room.

DA: What techniques and processes have you found to be successful in developing programs and working with the public in the roles you've had in museums?

CJ: A significant part of my process is acknowledging all the things I don't know and looking to those who do. Volunteers, staff in all departments, a regular who I know loves a particular kind of topic. Knowledge is everywhere and everyone has something to offer. Giving credit, asking permission, and giving back are essential to creating an accessible and equitable experience.

When developing programming, I gather as much insight from others as I can and ask for honest feedback. It can be easy for me to isolate when I'm in a position to write curriculum, but I am getting in the practice of never writing or prototyping programming completely by myself. I seek out several people to look over my work and provide feedback and new ideas and ask a lot of questions.

*Would you really enjoy sitting through this with your toddler? When I say this thing about gravity, do I need to elaborate? Is this prop distracting? How would you do this? If there was a class/show/experience here about X, what would you hope to do? You're right, I didn't take into consideration, X. How can I do better?*

I SIT IN THE SPACE WHERE I HOPE TO HOLD THE PROGRAM AND TAKE IN ALL THE DETAILS I CAN: *What are all my senses doing? Can I focus? Is the lighting too bright? Am I providing options that are outside assumed norms? If I do not live that experience, who or what resource can I consult that will inform my pedagogy and delivery?*

*What if a kiddo needs the bathroom all of a sudden? Why don't we keep a backup Mastodon tooth in here? What if no one laughs at my opening pun? How did this priceless 17th-century item get bent like that and do they even make these anymore?* These questions too, cause, you know, museum things.

I practice several ways of delivery. It's never enough to just write down everything you know about something and say it to someone who enters your exhibit. There is an art to communicating what a learning outcome is, being open to having to reframe that in the moment and being okay when things don't go as planned.

I watch my audience: body language, vocal reactions (why is no one gasping at my amazing use of liquid nitrogen!?), who is stopping to explore, who is just passing by, how faces change when I reveal an object. Smiling and making eye contact. Feeling my feet sink into the floor when I need grounding. Changing how I phrase things constantly. Noticing when someone is leaning in because they can't quite hear me or they need to leave because a kiddo is getting tired and signaling to them that it's okay.

Being upfront about my own identities is critical to delivery as well. If I'm speaking to something I cannot experience, I begin with that. I recently worked at a museum where we frequently gave tours on the history of race in the United States. I always began my tours by "pulling the cat out of the bag" (opening with a pun is always advisable), and addressing that as a white person, I cannot relate to the personal and lived experiences of racism that will come up for some participants. It was important to make clear my role was to know the specific exhibit, answer questions related to it and provide guiding questions for experiencing the space itself, not to bring my identities into a space where they shouldn't be the focus.

Establishing ground rules or agreements with participants can improve any program. I open with them regardless of the length of a program, who is present, or what the topic is. *What is our goal for today? How can I best support you all? What does respect mean and look like for this space? What are some agreements you all need me to follow?*

One of the agreements I always make with myself before I get to work is that I will have learned something new by the end of the day. Some days it's how I can do better tomorrow. Luckily, it tends to often be a story about a human connection that made my day or why I'm so excited to stay up all night researching something a guest shared with me.

It's also okay and really important to be honest with others about when you are in need of something too. When educating or working in customer service, whether in public space or not, there is often an expectation to "be on" and put aside our own emotional, spiritual, and physical needs even when we really need something. If my arthritis or other chronic pain symptoms are flaring up after a long day and I will occasionally need to sit down during a tour, I let my guests know, "there are chairs throughout the tour that can be sat in. I will be sitting in them when I need to today and you are welcome to use them too." I include as part of my introduction to any program information about places to sit, where restrooms are and encourage people to ask me to adjust my pacing, repeat something, or find out the answer to what I don't know with them later.

Validating all identities and experiences and having processes and expectations in place for both those who visit your museum and the folks who work there, is beneficial for everyone.

DA: What successes or challenges have you had in working with community?

CJ: On a daily basis, I try to measure success moment by moment and not get as caught up in quantitative data. While I realize there is a need for it and gather as much as possible when necessary (hello grant writing!), so much of the work that happens in informal education is incredibly experiential. I measure a lot via story and storytelling. The stories we tell about our spaces and how we exist in them and what we love about them can be a great measure of success.

One of my first museum jobs was at an outdoor park. Not unlike a lot of museum education work, they needed someone right away. I was there, enthusiastic and up for a challenge so I was flung into the outdoors to figure it out. I had 30 minutes to light a fire in the snow and it was terrifying. I cursed and cried and ripped my costume and worried the rest of the day that I had done something wrong and would burn the place down. When the fire began to lessen and the food I was cooking with learners turned out cold and with too much salt, community members, chaperones, and teachers were upset and frustrated. I wanted to quit that day and never come back. A community member offered to help and got my fire back up and running without judgment and we made another batch of food.

The story I told myself that day was that I wasn't meant to be a public educator, that guests or learners would never listen to me and that I should give up on my job. Several years later, I have learned from many more challenges, listened to members of my museum family and community at large when they recommended I do something differently, and found other ways to improve my skills outside of the field.

Today my stories are about how much I love museums and can't imagine doing anything else. I know that there are a lot of ways to correct something in the moment or change the course of a program and no longer experience stress in those situations. I also can light a fire in all kinds of conditions without much kindling like a pro, so bring it on, zombie apocalypse.

In a big picture sense, there will always be challenges that feel complex. The more museums stand with communities and their histories and their realities, the more we are going to have to face what it means to disrupt social norms and systems designed to hold people in struggle. If your museum is planning on returning cultural resources that have been in your space for a long time to a descendant community, as a couple museums I have worked with have, you have to prepare to field outrage, train and support staff and volunteers who will be engaging about the decision with the public, make your policy changes visible and accessible to everyone, and defend the descendant community first and foremost. Be prepared to apologize and take direction and set aside ego.

Museums have a long history of enabling the public to feel entitled to cultural resources, sacred traditions and knowledge that aren't theirs. Continuing to do so without the consent of the community they come from is a colonial practice, and changing this is necessary to create even more community relations for the future.

Engaging in practices of returning cultural resources to descendant communities or museums that are managed by and for the community they came from and updating your language museum-wide to include pronouns and hosting events that are focused on the often invisible history of certain communities, *is* caring about history and human survival and sustainability, and if your organization can't do that, what are you really standing for?

A challenge is an opportunity to grow, and I'm proud to have worked for spaces that realize they can't grow if they aren't being challenged and held accountable to change outdated ways of being and "knowing" about the field. The success of this is for the benefit of several generations from now and how hopefully, museums can be not just a third space, but really feel like home for many identities. Luckily, there are a lot of museums already creating and being this!

DA: Is there anything else that might be useful or interesting for other museum professionals to know if they were to attempt to work with their own community and develop a greater understanding of their identities vis-à-vis their museum and community?

CJ: Learn more about yourself and get to know your own identities and your museum space! Knowing the history of our spaces enables us to take ownership for what has happened there and plan how we want to make reparations for a better future.

Keep up on what other museums are doing to increase equity and support organizations run by and for from socially excluded communities already doing the work. Think outside of what you are already doing, don't just plan programs you would personally be interested in. If your organization is not already, support other museums that are run by and for people of color and LGBTQ+ folks and disabled folks, financially and by showing up and by recommending those spaces to your guests. Examine honestly what the identity makeup of your organization looks like and question why certain folks are missing or hiding themselves. Listen to community members when they critique or question an exhibit or program. Learn from it and do better. People are more important than ego.

I work in a lot in historic houses and spaces that are moving away from just being the site of where a wealthy, white family lived over a hundred years ago and it's for the better! Being able to have conversations about history as it relates to oppression and the realities of things that impact community identities today is not only vital for community at large, but vital for museum survival.

Have your staff and volunteers write love letters to themselves and their identities and to your museum. Connect personally and internally to why you love what you do and why your work matters. It does matter. You matter. Museums are amazing, and transformation is happening and always on the horizon.

## Museum of Anthropology in Vancouver

On September 21, 2018, I spoke with Jennifer Kramer, a curator at the Museum of Anthropology at the University of British Columbia (MOA) in Vancouver, British Columbia. Kramer eloquently describes the value and moral imperative of decolonization and authentic community partnership.

DA: Tell me about how you work with your community?

JENNIFER KRAMER (HEREAFTER REFERRED TO AS JK): Our museum resists "best practices" because best practices suggest that there is one solution for how a museum should work with all communities. At MOA, we feel that each relationship between the museum and a community is unique. Further relationships are really only between people, not between institutions, governing bodies, or abstract groups. Usually a relationship originates when an artist or a community member reaches out to the museum to start a conversation or vice versa. Working together comes down to trust. We have the experience to know that relationships change over time depending on context, the specific individuals involved, and their various goals or agendas. While many museums favor the model of having an Indigenous advisory board, at MOA we do not have consensus-based representational groups. We assume that individuals or self-representing communities will want to work with us in their own ways. Thus, an exchange begins.

DA: What is the exchange about?

JK: Often we are contacted by an individual who is connected to a specific object or objects in our museum because they are related to the "community of origin," i.e. the social group who commissioned its creation. These objects are masks, headdresses, talking sticks or other regalia that are material representations of supernatural or historical events connected to specific families or clans. When they are displayed during potlatches on the Northwest Coast of British Columbia, they are proof of sovereignty and resource rights. Potlatches were significant political, social, economic and ceremonial occasions that were outlawed in Canada between 1884 and 1951, but are on the rise again. Indigenous people are researching their family-owned privileges and intangible rights still embodied within these objects. MOA supports this important work. We want Indigenous voices and agendas to drive what we do. In fact, we don't use the term "artifacts" or talk of "collections"; instead we try to reflect Indigenous ways of thinking about these objects as "belongings" or "treasures" that do significant identity constituting. Thus, we consider ourselves stewards for communities. The language we use reflects the relationship we want to have with community.

We see ourselves as a nexus of knowledge exchange, but not a center. Our primary stakeholders are the First Nations of the Northwest Coast of Canada, but we want to be a place of value for all communities of origin, and we steward material culture from around the world. We want to be accessible to communities first, then we consider guest needs. But communities often consciously use the Museum as a place to represent themselves to others, so MOA becomes a place of cross-cultural interaction.

We are an urban museum in Vancouver. People can come and learn about contemporary lives of Indigenous people, both rural and urban. We strive to co-curate exhibitions about Indigenous art and culture. For example, MOA recently co-created with Indigenous curators from six different First Nations the exhibition "Culture at the Centre: Honouring Indigenous Culture, History, and Language." This exhibit brought together themes of common concern to Indigenous communities on the Northwest Coast today, such as land and reconciliation. We recognize both the right to self-representation and Indigenous copyright. Our partnerships can run the gamut from fully engaged to less engaged but we strive for the former. It depends on community interest and who is involved. It is important to know who you are speaking to and whether they speak for just themselves or larger groups, such as family, clan or First Nation. There is often pressure put on Indigenous artists to speak for their Nation, but many are not comfortable with this responsibility.

DA: Tell me about how you start communication with community members and groups?

JK: As I said, sometimes people contact us and sometimes we reach out, depending on the project to be developed, whether a public program, an exhibition, a community loan or a repatriation. We acknowledge there is always power at play. The first step is contact with individuals and figuring out whether we share mutual agendas or goals. We want the museum to be an open space that is welcoming.

We have two online, digital databases—The Reciprocal Research Network (RRN) and the MOA Collections Access Terminals (CAT). The RRN was co-developed with three First Nations and brings together Indigenous Northwest Coast material culture from 28 different holding institutions, and the MOA CAT offers images and catalogue information for our entire object holdings virtually. Not everyone can travel to the Museum, so we want to be as accessible as possible.

We aim to match ethics with products. The process of engagement that we use is just as significant as the product whether exhibition, public program or publication. Relationships of trust are so important. We try to learn every time and every time we do it, it gets smoother.

DA: What advice might you have for other museums who are trying to do this sort of work?

JK: Before you plan a project such as a grant application, exhibition, or education program, start with community from the beginning. You'll need to think through what this will mean for your timeline. Yes, it will take longer. It is so important to match community goals with museum goals because we want these to reflect and reinforce each other. Just doing the work of relationship building is crucial.

DA: Tell me about some of the difficulties you have had along the way as you work with First Nations.

JK: As part of our Renewal Project "A Partnership of Peoples: new infrastructure for collaborative research" the Museum re-organized our visible storage by working with Indigenous communities to find out how they would like their belongings and treasures displayed in the museum on public view. In 2010 we opened the revitalized "Multiversity Galleries" that utilized classification systems that make the most sense to the communities of origin with whom we worked. Multiversity refers to "many ways of knowing," as opposed to a university, which means "one way of knowing." As we quickly realized that there is no neutral way to organize, display or represent material culture, we instead emphasized Indigenous values and cosmological beliefs that were self-selected systems of knowing. We wanted the visible storage of Museum collections to reflect these values. We also started with indigenous languages as the first description on the object labels whenever possible. The Multiversity Galleries has embedded research rooms so that First Nations and other communities of origin can think about themselves as museum researchers and as partakers of cultural knowledge not passive viewers. The impetus comes from them.

These kinds of relationships keep going and blossoming—the Museum especially likes loaning out pieces back to Indigenous communities for ceremonial use. This helps us be a place that is meaningful to Indigenous people, and we are part of revitalization and cultural strengthening activities. We engage in exciting relationships that grow over time. Relationships will stop and start, but you never know where they will lead. The process is so important, because we learn from these engagements. We know that connection to culture, language, and community brings wellness. The core result of art creation and display can be reconciliation.

It is important for us as a museum made up of individuals to acknowledge that we can make missteps, but it's essential to try again. We have to be able to say, "I screwed up, but let's try again." And work together.

## Community work in Australia

The Bonegilla Migrant Reception and Training Centre in New South Wales, Australia, provides a fascinating case study around challenging history and memory as interpreted and received by community at museums. Bonegilla was a reception point and housing location for around 320,000 migrants and displaced individuals between 1947 and 1971.[2] Since that time, exhibits at museums throughout Australia—notably the Melbourne Immigration Museum and the Albury Library Museum—have attempted to contextualize and provide narratives around Australia's migrant history through the stories of individuals and situations at Bonegilla.

In a 2014 article in *Museums and Social Issues: A Journal of Reflective Practice*, Alexandra Dellios argues that the national metanarratives—which are traditionally celebratory, rather than questioning—have driven most representations of Bonegilla in exhibitions, rather than local communities and the voices of migrants who themselves spent time at the site.[3] Driven by high-dollar sponsors and government interests, these sorts of exhibits do not connect with the lived experience of community members and serve to stifle dialogue about the sometimes painful past. Alternatively, a website—Bonegilla.com—provides a Memories

Database for individuals who experienced Bonegilla to share their stories. In contrast to the museum exhibitions, this forum provides community members with opportunities to create their own meaning in a fluid and dynamic way.[4] Clearly, community engagement happens most effectively when the voices of the people most directly impacted by the events and places interpreted are both allowed and encouraged to contribute to meaning-making.[5]

## What can we learn from these case studies?

We first heard from Cassie Chinn at the Wing Luke Museum. With a long-running community engagement program to aid exhibit development, Chinn emphasized the importance of transparent and continuous communication. It's clear that maintaining good relationships in the community is taken seriously at the Wing Luke. Their staff do not just set up a panel or advisory group, get some feedback, and then send them on their way. Rather, they check in and double back to individuals in the community constantly. This ensures that the final product—exhibits and programs—are aligned with the needs, hopes, and dreams of the people who care so passionately about the art and history on display at the Wing Luke.

Next, we benefitted from Tine Van Goethem's experience with the *Yo!* exhibit at Bozar Centre for Fine Arts. Van Goethem shared how institutional timelines can clash with people who resist being institutionalized and highlighted the value of true dialogue that starts from a place of equal footing. What a valuable lesson for museum workers! It is so easy to place ourselves "above the fray" in our cultural and intellectual ivory towers. Van Goethem encourages us to climb down from those towers and to engage with our community face-to-face and democratically. Would that all museums could do this difficult and humbling work as well as Bozar did with the *Yo!* exhibit.

In a wide-ranging discussion, Franklin Cruz described the dangers of professionalism and Eurocentric mindsets in museums. He also drew attention to the value of using all of the creative tools at our disposal to design effective experiences. Content trapped in silos cannot be free to breathe the fresh air of the idiosyncratic ways in which our minds actually understand the world. We use all of our senses every day in concert with our brain to make sense of the world around us. Why would we want to stymie the beauty and insights into the human condition that we can have from interdisciplinary exploration? Museums must embrace Cruz's radical cross-pollination to maintain their vibrancy.

Cat Jensen delved into how our identity shapes either the joy or the sorrow that we find in museums. A thoughtful reflection on who we are as individuals gives us the liberty to then shape how our identity and the identities of those who come to our museums can rise together to create wondrous new pathways toward social justice. The work of museums cannot be done effectively without the sort of transparent reliance on truth and reflection that Jensen describes.

Jennifer Kramer from the Museum of Anthropology (MOA) in Vancouver exhorted us to cede control and to co-create and co-curate with traditionally neglected and wronged community groups. Kramer focused on how MOA has stopped to listen and to partner with First Nations in their area. The value of continuous learning and growth throughout these partnerships cannot be overstated. It is far easier to claim victory after an exhibit opening without critical reflection. But Kramer begged us to stop for a moment to learn from our missteps before we spring toward our next project. This advice is difficult, but so valuable for museums. We become inured to our community and walled off from reconciliation when we neglect to acknowledge and apologize for our mistakes.

Lastly, the Bonegilla Migrant Centre case study from Australia revealed the importance of providing forums for community dialogue around difficult history. Community groups and individuals want to tell their stories. Museums must be ready to open our doors to encourage people to share their lives with us in the ways that are meaningful to them.

## Notes

1 See www.bozar.be/en/activities/128044-yo for more information from the Bozar website about this exhibit and programming around it. Accessed 6 Nov. 2018.

2 Dellios, Alexandra. "Exchanging Memories in the Australian Museum: Migrant Stories and Bonegilla Migrant Centre." *Museums & Social*

*Issues*, vol. 9, no. 1, 2014, pp. 34–55. doi: 10.1179/1559689314Z.00000000018.

3 Ibid.

4 Ibid.

5 Other examples of museums tackling controversial or difficult topics and history whilst also involving community can be found in David B. Allison's *Controversial Monuments and Memorials: A Guide for Community Leaders*. Lanham, MD: Rowman & Littlefield, 2018.

# 4 Comparing models of development

From appreciative inquiry to Stanford design thinking and other for-profit project management models, museums have a range of techniques from which to draw. Which is right for you? The community in which you find yourself should determine what tools to use and how to blend techniques. For most museums, there will not be a single silver bullet that leads to success. Rather, a combination of approaches will yield results. Once a foundation of audience responsiveness and partnership has been built, community work can proceed in a number of intriguing directions.

## Organizational leadership

Leaders set the tone and are often the spark that sends an organization toward more meaningful community engagement. The next section will attempt a definition of leadership as explicated by research around organizational life cycle, employee readiness, and characteristics of leaders. It is hoped that this research might move forward our understanding of the characteristics that might be most desirable for new leaders as well as clarify ways that leaders can push museums toward community involvement.

## Organizational lifecycle and its effect on leadership growth

Where an organization finds itself on the continuum of development plays a huge role in the ability of that organization to effectively cultivate new leaders. During times of rapid change, where adaptability, flexibility, and creativity are necessary for innovation to occur, less senior employees can step up to the challenges of the moment and prove their mettle. At times of organizational stasis or stability, youthful coordinators or managers may not be able to forge their skills in the crucible of change and will be less ready to take on leadership positions. More recently, organizational lifecycle has been defined as less linear than some may perceive—that is, an organization is not infinitely and linearly perfectible, but instead often takes numerous twists and turns throughout its history. Rochelle Bayers ("Leadership Style" 22), writes that, "Indeed, organizational metamorphosis is the oscillation between order and disorder that is chaos." Effective leaders must be able to navigate organizational schemas in times of calm and in times of chaos.

## Readiness of employees and leadership and characteristics of good leadership

The importance of understanding how and when to apply coaching, mentoring, and talent planning for employees cannot be understated. Leaders must be aware of the readiness of their employees in order to assess when the time is right to proceed with various supervisory approaches. Hersey and Blanchard in *Bizjournal* (2013) describes readiness thusly: "Within the context of Situational Leadership, readiness is described as the ability and motivation of an employee toward a given task." Determining ability and motivation, then, becomes the primary challenge for leaders as they look toward developing employees within their organization.

Many studies have shown that individuals with an overly autocratic or process-oriented approach are demotivating for their employees. When a supervisor demonstrates that they do not trust their employees through rampant, highly detailed questioning and through "micromanaging," employees begin to feel like they are not empowered to do the work that they have the skills to handle. In addition, individuals who are unable to "see the forest for the trees" can often get bogged down in the minutiae of the work to the detriment of the organization's overall direction.

## The importance of considering all determinants of leadership

Leadership is not static. The needs of the organization and the needs of employees are in constant flux, which requires a keen attention to all the factors that may influence the success of various leadership styles at any given moment. Sometimes a strong hand with radical candor and brutally honest feedback is necessary to move an organization forward. At other times, an empathetic, caring approach can serve to connect employees to each other and will spur organizational success in new ways. Locking in to one leadership technique will serve only to calcify business practices and will strand an organization on shoals of inertia and decay.

## Systems thinking as a method to improve organizational effectiveness

A system has been described by Ackoff ("Systems Thinking" 175) as a "whole that cannot be divided into independent parts or subgroups of parts." Ackoff's definition is helpful, as it is broad enough to encompass most aspects of everyday life and does not presuppose exclusively business or corporate applications. Building upon Ackoff's perspicacious and comprehensive definition, this section will explore both closed and open systems and will provide a definition of both of these as well as an overview of systems thinking. In addition, we will distinguish between hard systems thinking and soft systems thinking whilst explaining the performance of systems.

When exploring systems, it is helpful to distinguish between open and closed systems. An open system is one that can be influenced by external forces and is able to be impacted by what is happening outside the strictures of the day-to-day internal processes and procedures (Ackoff 177). Alternately, a closed system is one in which there are no external influences and the system is totally unrelated to the environment around it. In a business context, a closed system would remain uninfluenced by a strategic foresight which seeks to understand the competition and business environment in which it functions. In my experience, closed systems have the advantage of being able to learn deeply from past experiences in order to inform the present. Closed systems rely upon what they know intimately and can become inward-looking and shut off from external influences over time as a result of this narrow range of experience.

Systems thinking is a way of solving problems through rational, step-by-step processes. It is important here to acknowledge that the systems thinking approach has its basis in the Enlightenment and modernist ideals around steady progress through rational decision-making (Jackson 66). As such, the conclusions that we draw from a systems approach are geared toward bettering the lives of the stakeholders involved. To explore an example from my work at the Denver Museum of Nature & Science, it can be seen that when all of the stakeholders were satisfied with a systems-based solution to developing a museum-wide calendaring system for scheduling space use and tracking events, the schoolchildren had more space for their stuff when they come in, guests for a fundraiser had more time to hobnob without interruptions, and staff members' stress level around booking spaces was minimized. A postmodernist critique of systems thinking would throw into question the idea that satisfaction for those individuals is even a goal to be achieved and would cause us to question whether or not it is even worth it to "upset the apple cart" through changes to calendaring structures if there can actually be no ultimate good for which to strive.

I hold out hope for humanity, however, and trust that rationality can lead to a better future for all stakeholders. The problem of multiple ways of tracking events and programs at the museum was effectively solved through a systems thinking approach which identified guiding principles around priorities and found an alternative tool for sharing calendar information across departments. Additionally, using systems thinking identified potential unforeseen outcomes of implementing the new calendaring tool.

Hard systems thinking and soft systems thinking can be differentiated by the degree to which they actually employ a process-driven approach to solving problems. In a hard systems thinking schema, problems are tackled from a "point A to point B" perspective, with clear solutions proposed to each problem in a fairly linear fashion. Soft systems feature a learning environment in which continual improvement is the goal in more of a looping, broadly interpreted fashion. Hard systems thinking can be applied effectively in situations like engineering firms that require very strict, repeatable solutions to problems. Soft systems thinking in more effective when the problem does not require an immediate solution or when it is complicated by human or societal structures that deserve a more evolutionary approach.

Systems performance is more than the sum of the performance of its parts. A clear, overarching vision or goal should unite a system and propel it toward functionality. Even if all the parts of a system are functioning well, they could be focused toward an unclear or wrong-headed goal that is at cross-purposes to an organization's mission or vision. In this sort of situation, a radical recalibration of the system is needed in order to get it back in line with the company's overarching goals.

## Duty of Care and organizational impact through human resources

The Duty of Care is a well-established principle that has been used as a way to encourage managers to provide benefits beyond health care and time off to their employees and improve their "quality of life" at the company. Contrasted with this duty (which is not a legal duty in the least) is the fiduciary duty of managers to the company, which may be strictly at odds with the principles of the Duty of Care.

This section will explore the nature and scope of the Duty of Care and will provide some key examples which might elucidate how this duty plays itself out in a company. Then we will transition to an exploration of how the legal fiduciary duties may bump up against the ethical Duty of Care and propose for solutions for how these contrasting duties might be reconciled or mitigated.

Ultimately it is in the interest of the employer to have employees who feel taken care of and happy in their employment. They will work harder and be more loyal to the company as a result of the connection that they feel to their employer. Of course, it is important to acknowledge that there is a difference between *care* and *coddling*—and employers must resist the temptation to start talking about a business environment as a "family," which it patently is not, and which can lead to inappropriate work relationships and an laissez-faire approach to supervision and corrective action.

As discussed and explored by Manuel G. Velasquez in *Business Ethics: Concepts and Cases*, the potentially troublesome aspects of work relationships that are too tightly intertwined can be quite deleterious for a company; "this is the problem of balancing partiality toward those for whom we care with the impartial demands of other moral considerations, such as the impartial demands of fairness or of moral rights" (448). It is much harder to draw firm lines in the sand around another person's actions when we care deeply about them in ways that stretch beyond traditional work relationships.

While companies should be wary of deep interpersonal connections between supervisors and supervisees, it is certainly incumbent upon corporations to provide care for their employees at some meaningful level—because it is the right and moral thing to do, but also because it will be hard to recruit and retain employees if the corporate culture is aggressively uncaring. There are multitudes of examples from companies that have been viewed as creating a cutthroat or difficult culture based on denigration and competition instead of positive reinforcement and empowerment. A recent noteworthy example is from Amazon, the huge multi-platform online retailer and technology company, which was exposed as having extremely difficult and intense working conditions—both for their warehouse workers (who often went without air conditioning even in the height of summer) and for their white-collar workers, who were asked to avoid vacations and time off and were bullied repeatedly—according to a *New York Times* article from August 15, 2015 (Kanter and Streitfeld).

The bad publicity alone for Amazon should cause other companies with similar approaches to their work culture to rethink their Duty of Care for their employees. Not only did Amazon come off as callous (which may have made consumers more sensitive about using their services and buying their products), but up-and-coming potential employees who may once have viewed working at Amazon as a great entrée into the technology world might now start to avoid the company as a result of this article. Good working conditions and reasonable expectations that allow for personal time should be key considerations for a company that desires to have a clear duty of care for its employees that is balanced with legal duties.

It is inevitable that sometimes ethical duties will conflict with legal duties in a business setting. When this happens, the judgments around the best course of action should come from a carefully considered set of expectations. These expectations should establish legal duties as sacrosanct and provide avenues for folding in ethical concerns with the undeniable legal imperatives of the company. Fiduciary duties are the most concrete example of a legal duty that will supersede ethical qualms, but that should certainly be balanced and thought about from both a human resources perspective as well as from a shareholder perspective alongside ethical considerations.

Another response that should be considered when legal and financial duties come into conflict with ethical duties is for the director team to provide adequate training and mentoring based in case studies around ethical and legal duties. Training of this type will support employees as they make decisions, whilst also mitigating liability in the eventuality of a lawsuit. Managers and workers alike will greatly benefit from a corporate culture which has open communication around ethical and legal considerations in the workplace—not doing so could be considered a neglect of the Duty of Care.

Concern and care for employees is absolutely imperative for companies in the increasingly globalized business climate of the late 2010s. Corporations that are unable to balance their legal duties with a clear ethical responsibility for their workers risks marginalization and loss of market share. It is not merely a matter of doing the right thing—it is a matter of survival.

## Teams

Teams are as divergent and varied as the individuals who populate them. Peter Drucker ("Drucker on Management") argued that there are, at the core, only three different types of teams, but that these team types are highly distinctive and should be applied in specific contexts to solve the sticky organizational situations that they are designed to tackle. This section will explore some of the primary models that business theorists have posited around team leadership and will present some "lived experience" around the effectiveness of teams.

### *"Baseball" team model explained*

In Drucker's schema ("Drucker on Management"), the three distinct types of teams (baseball, football, and tennis doubles) can be considered to be "tools" that should be applied in different situations depending on the needs of the business at the time. The first type of team is the baseball team, which refers to a group of individuals who all have distinct skills that are applied at different times to solve one problem. A real-world example of this type of team would be from a hospital surgical team, where the nurse performs one role and the anesthesiologist performs an entirely separate one. While each member of this sort of team communicate with each other, they are connected together only by the end goal. The strength of this approach lies in the leveraging of the unique skills of each individual. Most literature, however, has looked askance at the "siloed" work styles of this team model (Drucker).

### *"Football" team model explained*

The football team model provides more rigidity than baseball teams—they have individuals who are performing specific roles, and these individuals are all working toward a common goal, but one strictly defined by the "playbook" that explains how each individual is to work together to win the game. The business analogue for the football team model would be a Japanese automaker's design teams, which consist of teams constructed around hewing closely to streamlined processes through flexible design schemas and well-scoped work constraints (Drucker).

### *"Tennis doubles" team model explained*

In Drucker's tennis doubles model, individuals have a "primary" role or responsibility, but they cover for each other and know how to perform the key functions of their fellow teammates. This type of team is considered to be the best for promoting innovation, as often the solutions that can arise from the combined efforts of multiple people can be more insightful and advantageous than solutions that might emerge from an individual in a vacuum performing a very specific function. This type of team is exemplified by most of the personal computer companies, which value innovation more than almost any other skillset.

While Drucker's three models all have their advantages and disadvantages, it seems clear that each one can be applied at different times for different reasons. The Druckerian models do not, however, address some of the many relational advantages of teams, which I have experienced in my own career. As described by Musselwhite ("Building and Leading High Performing Teams"), teams that have effective facilitated interactions and solid communication based on well-understood and agreed-upon goals end up being the most successful. Teams based on trust and a common vision can rise to meet almost any challenge and have been able to effectively adapt their practices to include community more intimately.

## Being a learning organization

A learning organization is signified by a focus on nimbleness and questioning of assumptions as a way to work toward ongoing improvement throughout the various aspects of the business. The term "learning organization" is fairly new on the business scene, and it gained significant cache only in the early 1990s (Kim and Senge 280). Despite its relative youth, it is a helpful concept for organizations to strive for as a part of their efforts to gain a competitive advantage. This section will explore what organizational learning is as well as define what a learning organization is. In addition, the organizational learning cycle will be explained in some depth, as well as some potential roadblocks to organizational learning that may throw a wrench into the learning cycle.

Garvin ("Building a Learning Organization") has identified five main activities at which learning organizations are skilled: systematic problem solving, experimentation with new approaches, learning from their own experience and past history, learning from the experiences and best practices of others, and transferring knowledge quickly and efficiently throughout the organization. These five activities provide the basis upon which a learning organization can create new ideas—an essential component of learning.

When human beings learn something, they scaffold new information onto their prior knowledge so that they can then use that information in productive, useful ways. The same applies to organizational learning. The point of organizational learning is to enable a company to reach into new realms of success by finding better ways of doing business both external and internal to their company. The purpose of organizational learning is to actually implement the new ideas, rather than merely gather data or embark upon benchmarking (Garvin 83). In the museum world, there are vastly different types of content being presented—art, science, and history, to name a few. Yet, all museums must find ways to share their content with the public in ways that will be interesting and engaging to their audience. Therefore, the more that museums can look "outside themselves" to experience providers of all stripes (rather than only other museums), the better they will be able to differentiate themselves and serve the unique communities in which they exist. Museums, therefore, would benefit from becoming learning organizations in much the same way that for-profit enterprises have.

When considering organizational learning, it is helpful to view it as going through specific cycles that create the distinct "back and forth" and response to new knowledge acquisition that should be the hallmark of efficacious organizations. A model in which actions of an individual result in organizational actions would start from a place of inquisitiveness about both the internal systems of an organization as well as the external environment in which a company finds itself (Goh 16). Following from this baseline, the learning by the organization would result in actions and steps taken to respond to these learnings. The final part of the cycle, then, is the response from the "marketplace" or external environment, which should impact individual learning. As individuals learn, the organization will also gain institutional memory, thus completing the cycle (Goh 17).

As in any process that involves humans and organizations, there are several potential roadblocks that can hinder the transformation of a business into a learning organization throughout the cycle described above. A key roadblock to the organizational learning cycle is the interference of upper management, who may fear close scrutiny of their actions and desire to hold on to the trappings of power. Another roadblock may be faulty data or information from external sources that may not actually be relevant to the cycle. Another roadblock may be apathy on the part of employees who do not wish to put in the requisite effort required to truly learn from the internal systems and external environment in order to transform the organization. Each of these roadblocks can be overcome through thoughtful change management that seeks to honor the contributions and ideas that may emerge from all aspects of the organization. There is no silver bullet for success, however, and each organization must be able to identify the potential roadblocks within their organization and be ready to bust through them with thoughtful relationship-building and systems thinking. Interestingly, some recent thinking about learning organizations has shown that when businesses have been able to track and benchmark their progress toward becoming a learning organization, they have been able to more effectively pitch changes across all levels of the company (Garvin et al.). It is important not only to embark upon the learning and self-examination, but to show its value through systematic reporting structures.

## What is shared value?

Implementing a shared value approach to capitalism can also bring organizations in alignment with their community. Organizations that have been able to strategically position themselves to be leaders in the field and to maintain their edge as top-notch employers who offer amazing opportunities for professional development to our talented team have been able to work more closely with community. Shared value is the transformative approach to business that can vault organizations forward into the increasingly connected and socially conscious 21st century. Simply put, shared value elevates the idea of social purpose as a key aspect of a capitalist society. Businesses that embrace shared value do so not only out of a desire to build goodwill and a better image amongst the public, but also as a way to truly effect change and meet the needs of society in a meaningful way.

## Readings and resources to understand shared value

Perhaps the seminal article about shared value comes from Michael Porter and Mark Kramer in "Creating Shared Value" (2011), which argues that the concept of shared value is the most effective approach to addressing seemingly intractable social problems like poverty, hunger, and disease through an entrepreneurial mindset that identifies needs and seeks to fulfill these needs through market-driven solutions. Porter expanded on this idea in his interview with Michaela Driver in 2012 by describing shared value as "a permanent shift toward the pursuit of *higher profits* [emphasis his], that is, profits that also produce positive social change, and financial markets that reward companies for doing just that" (Interview with Michael Porter" 422). This quote not only advocates for individual companies shouldering a shared value model but also makes it clear that no lasting transformation can take place without the buy-in from a wider group of companies who must work in concert to remake the markets away from the profit maximization relics of the 19th and 20th centuries, which sought for profits at all costs and toward a model which values societal advancement and broad-based "wins."

While these platitudes may sound nice in theory, it is important to determine just what this might look like in practice. One article which explores shared value in action is from L. Vaidyanathan and M. Scott called "Creating Shared Value in India" (2012). Vaidyanathan and Scott note that Hindustan Unilever Lifebuoy soap realized that by reconceiving the market for hygiene products and promoting better health, they could actually find a more willing market for their soap, whilst also decreasing the incidences of diarrhea in India—a particularly pernicious scourge in that country (Vaidyanathan and Scott 110).

Non-profits have realized that large societal problems like poverty and a failing educational system are too difficult for individual organizations to tackle on their own and have started to turn to a concept known as "collective impact." The same Mark Kramer from the "Creating Shared Value" piece wrote an article aimed at non-profits in the *Stanford Social Innovation Review* with John Kania ("Collective Impact"), which describes how non-profits can start to turn the tide against these societal ills by uniting with a number of other non-profits in a locality (typically a city) around some shared goals and metrics for what will move the needle on a given social problem and then individually pursuing their own solutions via the tools that best align with their mission and competencies. This approach capitalizes on the "market strengths" of each non-profit as they pursue a common goal, but use divergent approaches to achieving that goal.

With shared value instead of corporate social responsibility, there is no trade-off of profitability in the pursuit of the right thing to do. Rather, organizations can enhance their bottom line through identifying the needs of society and devising entrepreneurial solutions that honor the traditions and values of the places in which we do business. From that basis, organizations can work to reshape markets and carve out a place for themselves that both help to make the world a better place and are also sustainable and profitable.

## Strategic context and performance improvement process

All organizations must be focused on their customers as a starting point for continuous improvement (Brassard and Ritter 155). Museums gather a plethora of customer feedback in the form of mystery shopper reports, customer surveys and evaluations, and analysis of data on visitation, ticket sales, and member metrics. The commitment to gathering copious input from customers is certainly laudable, yet that information can quickly become useless if it is not widely shared internally or approached as a cog in a holistic continuous improvement process.

A continuous improvement process has been defined in relation to organizations by Plenert (*Strategic Continuous Process Improvement* 7) as, "incorporating relentless improvement with a focus on business strategy." While Plenert's definition is a good starting place, I would posit that a sound continuous improvement process would also seek to be ecumenical in its exploration of a wide range of techniques and systems from best practices in other organizations. Locking ourselves into one system can create a poor match for an organization's culture, resulting in deleterious effects that may cripple the organization, rather than enhance its effectiveness.

## Tools for transformation—models of development

The bottom line for museums is providing great experiences for our customers. Most organizations are littered with potentially great ideas to enhance their reputation or reach that have fallen by the wayside due to a failure to pay attention to customers and to improve their performance through a systematic approach. When museums put customers at the forefront of decision-making, then we can confidently seek out the best tools from businesses and other organizations to create consistently high-quality experiences that are adaptable to the ever-changing business and cultural environment of our increasingly globalized and connected world. In doing so, we ready ourselves to engage with our community.

At the Denver Museum of Nature & Science, we have found that a combination of Stanford Design Thinking approach and Appreciative Inquiry is most effective for project and program development. Design thinking identifies user needs through empathy interviews and then, after developing a "how might we . . ." statement, embarks upon rapid prototyping and iteration. This process yields fast feedback on products in the design phase.

DMNS pairs design thinking with appreciative inquiry—a technique that seeks to identify the positive aspects within a system in order to uncover how organizations can build on those strengths rather than lapse into a hopeless sort of deficit thinking that curtails creative solutions. Appreciative Inquiry relies on layered interviews—"discovery"—that build toward "dream"—which envisions what could be in the future. Dream and discovery then lead to "design"—a very similar phase to the prototyping of design thinking, and then end with "destiny"—putting the three previous phases into tangible action. Both of these techniques require some training to effectively implement. I would encourage you to seek out trainers and workshops on these techniques so that your staff are equipped to listen, innovate, and partner hand-in-hand with community.

## Key references

Ackoff, Russell. "Systems Thinking and Thinking Systems." *Systems Dynamics Review*, vol. 10, nos. 1–2, 1994, pp. 175–186.

Bayers, Rochelle. "Leadership Style and the Organization Lifecycle." MA diss., Adler Graduate School, 2011.

Brassard, Michael, and Diane Ritter. *The Memory Jogger: Tools for Continuous Improvement and Effective Planning*. 2nd ed., Salem: Goal/QPC, 2010.

Brown, Tim. *Change by Design: How Design Thinking Transforms Organizations and Inspires Innovation*. New York: Harper Business, 2009.

Buell, John M. "Living the Organization's Mission, Vision, and Values." *Healthcare Executive*. Nov./Dec. 2008, p. 21.

Cooperrider, David and Diane Whitney. *Appreciative Inquiry: A Positive Revolution in Change*. San Francisco, CA: Berrett-Koehler Publishers, 2008.

Driver, Michaela. "Interview with Michael Porter." *Academy of Management Learning and Education*, vol. 11, no. 3, 2012, pp. 421–431.

Drucker, Peter. "Drucker on Management: There is More than One Kind of Team." *Wall Street Journal*. 2009. www.wsj.com/articles/SB100014420430457454431291627742. Accessed 10 Apr. 2016.

Garvin, David. "Building a Learning Organization." *Harvard Business Review*, vol. 71, no. 4, Jul./Aug. 1993, pp. 78–91.

Garvin, David, et al. "Is Yours a Learning Organization?" *Harvard Business Review*, Mar. 2008, pp. 109–116.

Goh, Swee. "Toward a Learning Organization: The Strategic Building Blocks." *SAM Advanced Management Journal*, vol. 63, no. 2, Spring 1998, pp. 15–22.

Hopkins, Michael. "How SAP Made the Business Case for Sustainability." *MIT Sloan Management Review*, vol. 52, no. 1, 2010, pp. 69–72.

Jackson, Mike. "Beyond the Fads: Systems Thinking for Managers." *Systems Research*, vol. 12, no. 1, 1995, pp. 25–42.

Kania, John, and Mark Kramer. "Collective Impact." *Stanford Social Innovation Review*, Winter 2011, pp. 36–41.

Kanter, James, and David Streitfeld. "Inside Amazon: Wrestling Big Ideas in a Bruising Workplace." *New York Times*, Aug. 15, 2015. www.nytimes.com/2015/08/16/technology/inside-amazon-wrestling-big-ideas-in-a bruising-workplace.html. Accessed 10 Oct. 2015.

Kim, Daniel, and Senge, Peter. "Putting Systems Thinking into Practice." *Systems Dynamics Review*, 10 (2 / 3), Summer/Fall 1994, pp. 277–290.

Mallor, Jane, James A. Barnes, Thomas Bowers, and Arlen W. Langvardt. *Business Law: The Ethical, Global and E-commerce Environment*. 15th ed., New York: McGraw-Hill, 2013.

Musselwhite, Charlie. "Building and Leading High Performing Teams." *Inc. Magazine*, 2007. www.inc.com/resources/leadership/articles/20070101/musselwhite.html. Accessed 10 Apr. 2016.

Plenert, Gerhard. *Strategic Continuous Process Improvement*. New York: McGraw Hill, 2012.

Porter, Michael, and Mark Kramer. "Creating Shared Value." *Harvard Business Review*, Jan.–Feb. 2011, pp. 62–77.

Vaidyanathan, Lalitha, and Melissa Scott. "Creating Shared Value in India." *Vikapia*, vol. 37, 2012, pp. 108–113.

Velasquez, Manuel G. *Business Ethics: Concepts and Cases*. 7th ed., London: Pearson, 2004.

# 5 Staying connected with community

When the dust has settled and the daily grind of everyday programming and operations reasserts itself, how do we make the relationships forged in moments of great excitement or special projects continue? How do we sustain high-level partnerships over time? What do long-term partnerships look like as business imperatives morph for museums? Once museums have established relationships with other organizations and within the community, it is important to take the right steps in order to ensure that these partnerships stay strong.

Each museum has unique challenges, unique stories to tell, unique collections, and a unique community in which it operates. An analogy for our community work is adult coloring books. We choose the colors we want to use and decide what designs we might want to add within the lines. But the picture is already there, with guidance for where to put the colors. The good news for us is that we already have a picture that has been drawn and identified by our history and our community. We need to exercise our creativity within those lines. It sounds easier than it actually is, but it is essential to keep within the lines we developed in conjunction with our partners in order to continue to meet audience needs.

As we turn to trusted partners over long periods of time, we find that the barriers that once existed have become stepping stones toward greater impact. We learn about new skills and competencies that the organization or person has that can be applied in new ways with us. They introduce us to their friends and partners, and our networks grow. Sustained partnerships lead to the infusion of new relationships that provide a buffer against the inertia of insular navel-gazing. Constantly being introduced to new partners means that we have to be ever at the ready to start new processes and procedures that will help us to make connections in rejuvenated ways. What might have worked with one partner will almost certainly not work in the same way with a new partner. We are all individuals with unique needs and ideas, and so to try to fit the old processes that worked with one partner onto a new relationship will likely result in miscommunication and misunderstanding. The only true remedy for the rut of tired processes is to approach new relationships with a flexibility of mind and openness to reinvention.

I have mowed many lawns. I started mowing when I was 14 and quickly branched out beyond our house to other yards in the neighborhood. Soon I had a burgeoning business in lawn mowing. Later, I got the job mowing the lawn at the neighborhood park.

Mowing is a relaxing activity. I shut down my mind and just auto-pilot the job. I can't hear anything other than the rumble of the engine, and the sweet grass smell is familiar and comforting. But I can remember one time when mowing a lawn was decidedly not relaxing. I was probably in college when this incident happened. I was hired to mow the neighbor's lawn across the street. Mr. Tolliver told me to be sure to check the lawn for any rocks or other obstacles before starting, but I scoffed at this idea. I'd been doing this for five years now and I always was able to just start it up and do it. So, heedless of his encouragement, I followed my typical routine—I prepped the lawn mower by making sure the tank was full and then pushed it across the street. After starting it up, I just blindly got to work and shut off my brain in my typical way. About halfway through the front yard, the mower jolted and the engine whined as I hit something that made a scrunching sound. As I leaned down to check the mower, a gaggle of angry bees flew up from under it. Quickly turning tail and running back across the street, I was stung multiple times before I finally made it into our house.

I realize now that during that incident, I fell into a fixed mindset instead of being open to new ways of doing things. I was stung by my own pride in my past successes as much as I was by the bees. I had been so sure of my way of doing things that I failed to listen to the good advice of someone who knew their yard much better than I did.

This is a lesson for us as well. It's easy to get stung when we dive in headfirst to new partnerships without taking the time to listen and respond appropriately. It's easy to find ourselves running away from situations that have gotten out of control when we neglect to stop and proceed with a dose of humility and caution.

A glance at how the Denver Museum of Nature & Science approaches long-term partnerships may be illustrative. The Denver-metro *Scientific and Cultural Facilities District* (SCFD) provides direct support for operations of the DMNS. Though not required by SCFD legislation, the DMNS conducts 12 Free Days and Nights ("Free Days") to acknowledge the generosity of the residents within the district in their approval of the sales tax.

SCFD Free Days and Nights ("Free Days") aim to increase accessibility and reduce economic barriers to the DMNS for our guests through free admission, with programming that reflects and celebrates our nearby community through partnerships and collaborations. Whether activities or performances, programming on Free Days is generally the "icing on the cake" for most visitors. Though not typical for a regular paid-admission day, programming on Free Days allows the Museum to channel requests from external organizations to exhibit their activities or performances on days that are already have committed staff resources to support special programs. Programming should generally align with DMNS values and areas of expertise. DMNS staff are diligent in conversations with partners to ensure that the following criteria is met:

- Be appropriate for family audiences, especially with considerations for safety
- Be highly interactive—create, build, play, learn
- Promote science, technology, engineering, the arts, or math
- Be free of charge to participate
- Do not directly promote the sale or marketing of any products or services

There are organizations with whom the DMNS has identified an intentional, long-term relationship that helps to advance each group's mission. In general, there is an assumption that we will continue to co-create programming with partners for one of the Free Days on an annual basis, unless the relationship changes. Partnerships are generally initiated from Museum leadership, though the day-to-day operations for Free Days lives with the Coordinator. The Museum has co-created free days in the past with the Mexican Cultural Center for Día del Niño, Americas for Conservation + the Arts (Americas Latino Eco Festival) and LGBTQ Community Partners (LGBT Center of Colorado, Gender Identity Center, OASOS/Out Boulder, LGBTQ Student Resource Center, PFLAG). All partnerships for Free Days are reconsidered each year with input from the Senior Leadership Team of the Museum.

The Museum also collaborates with partners. These are generally one-time, one-off programming from external organizations, though programming may be recurring from year to year. There is also strategic value in partnering with other SCFD organizations, especially smaller organizations, on Free Days. One example is the DMNS's collaboration with the Black American West Museum. Programming from the Black American West Museum and other collaborators is not co-created (though support may be provided to ensure that activities meet the DMNS's standards for high-quality, hands-on, and engaging programming), as groups come in with pre-formulated activities. Examples of past groups with whom the DMNS has collaborated with in the past for Free Day programming include the University of Colorado Denver Neuroscience Students, Regional Air Quality, and Shaak Music Studio.

From time to time, Free Days will have programming with organizations initiated through funding partners. These financial partnerships give the organizations an opportunity to conduct an activity, but do not constitute naming rights to the event. Free Days are sponsored only by SCFD. Funding partners are still expected to adhere to the activity standards of Free Days. DMNS also contracts with outside experience providers on Free Days to enhance what we offer for guests. Examples include face painters and musicians.

Where appropriate, programming will be focused on particular themes so as to create a cohesive experience for guests and to use the museum's resources efficiently. Themes may be driven by our community partners, may be created by the Free Day coordination team, or may be vestiges of past DMNS events that have traction with our audience. Because we already have staffing resources in place and the Museum has committed to support Free Days on a large scale, there is built-in efficiency in co-creating and partnering on Free Days. For example, when the LGBTQ community day was approved as an operationalized community activity, we decided that from a resource perspective it made sense to combine it with a community Free Day. When specific days are co-created with partners, these are advertised as such (e.g. Día del Niño, LGBTQ Community Day).

Free Days have continued to be successful at DMNS because partners and co-creators have been fully engaged over a long period of time with the Museum. Relationships of trust have been built because the Museum has ceded control and provided avenues for other organizations to take the lead in the development and execution of programming. Ongoing partnerships have yielded huge benefits for our audience through Free Days.

What unique and interesting partnerships might your museum be ready to begin? Building lasting relationships of trust and respect can start with a simple phone call or chat at an event and can blossom into the types of partnerships that drive organizational success. Seek out these partners everywhere and be open to being transformed by them.

## Tools for transformation—staying connected

Staying connected with partners mimics how we stay connected with our friends. Friends know that you care about them when you remember their birthday. They know that you want to stay in touch with them when you shoot them a text message out of the blue. Friendships are cultivated when you ask your pal to give you advice about a sticky problem you have been wrestling with.

Likewise, we need to reach out personally and frequently to our partners at other organizations to maintain strong connections. Attending functions and events in the community in the places where people gather and your partners do their work shows true commitment. The seemingly simple actions of sending an occasional “How are things going?” email and of remembering to invite contacts to soirees can sustain partnerships beyond the life of a one-off project. In addition, true investment in what really matters to your partners—even if you can't see immediate benefit for your organization—can lead to new ideas and new realms of engagement.

As you build your networks of partners, consider when it may be advantageous (or necessary) to reframe your relationship. Have you been mindlessly repeating the same sorts of activities with your program partner year after year as visitation slows and energy fades? If so, perhaps it's time to sit down with your partner and think creatively about how you work best together and what you might be able to do differently in the future to revivify your relationship. Partnerships must not become static. Without change and new ideas, our engagement with community becomes trapped in the amber of an aimless torpor and inertia.

## Key references

Golding, Viv, and Wayne Modest, editors. *Museums and Communities: Curators, Collections and Collaborations*. London: Bloomsbury Academic, 2013.

Simon, Nina. *The Participatory Museum*. Santa Cruz: Museum 2.0, 2010.

# Conclusion

## New pathways and ideas in museums

Looking beyond the realm of non-profits yields helpful lessons for how to craft intentional and emotionally resonant experiences. From immersive theatre to amusement parks to pop-up art installations, the world of experience design is large and constantly expanding. What might we learn from these diverse venues? Psychological comfort, starting with the heart before the brain and the importance of fun, repeatable shared experiences are techniques that can—and should—be borrowed from the "best of the best" in experience providers like Disney and Pixar.

As provocation, it is hoped that this book will encourage a search for purpose and a questioning of long-held assumptions and patterns. Start with why, identify what, and then build your "how" hand-in-hand with community.

The past few years have been incredibly painful. The world seems to spiral toward violence and we become numbed to the cycles of intolerance and hate that circle around us. The racist white supremacists who rallied in Charlottesville and the resulting death of Heather Heyer. The brutal killing of 11 worshipping Jews at a synagogue in Pittsburgh and, earlier, the murders of nine parishioners of the Emmanuel African Methodist Episcopal (AME) church in Charleston, South Carolina. The UN report in 2018 that the earth is on the brink of environmental collapse if humans do not start immediately to make changes to consumption and to take steps to staunch climate change. Balkanized politics threaten to overwhelm our sentiments.

When these incidents pile up and the temptation to inure ourselves begins to overwhelm us, the strength and beauty of relationships and the true nature of community can become a salve and a hope in the midst of darkness. We can see too that there must be a philosophical underpinning for this sort of community strength.

In the early 1960s, as America was forced to face the legacy of slavery and terror against black people, Civil Rights leaders articulated the concept of the beloved community. The beloved community became a diverse group of people united in their hope for a better future. They envisioned a future free of racism and the stifling segregation wrought by Jim Crow laws. At its core, the beloved community turned its eyes toward transformative hope and redemption to away the grime of the depths of hate that produced violence and inequality. By the end of the 1960s and the early 1970s, the shine of the beloved community had begun to fade as progress did not come quickly and as old coalitions within the Civil Rights Movement crumbled.

What if we brought back the beloved community?[1] Could we start such a movement in museums? We know definitively that museums are not (and can never be) apolitical. We function within the structures of our society, and we are beholden to the vagaries of politics every day. Funding sources are fragile. Powerful donors stand ready to either withhold or donate money.

Finding our own beloved community—a coalition of people and groups ready to engage with society around the issues that matter—can be our own answer to the galvanizing forces of white nationalism and climate change-deniers that gather at our doorstep. Our contemporary challenges—which span the globe—beg us to be clear about who we are and what we do. When we emerge with a clear mission and vision, we find that we become aligned with movements, people, and ideas that move us toward deeper and more meaningful relationships across the whole range of human experience and identities. This, then, is our contemporary beloved community.

Allies and friends can be everywhere as we root ourselves in our unique identities and push back against false understandings of history, science deniers, and the rising scourge of milquetoast relativism. The beloved community can regenerate the sickness of our culture and revivify the squalor of our souls. Finding this community must be our goal.

We stumble when we assume that we are the first to have ever struggled in this way. The human condition predates us and will postdate us as well. What do we do with the moments given us? Building into others' lives is more than good business practice. It is our way to understand and grapple with our humanity and to strive for something greater than petty corporeal jealousies and greed. Being shocked and scandalized by evil doesn't do a damn thing to fight it.

We need to move past cries of outrage and empty dialogue. Action that matters for the world can start with museums. We are trusted, safe places that offer people both sanctuary from chaos as well as a forum to open critical conversations. Embracing this role and standing and acting in our convictions will place museums in the middle of the stickiest problems facing society. That is precisely where we need to be.

## Note

1 After I wrote this chapter, I found that Mike Murawski independently suggested that museums should recapture this idea of the beloved community. His references to this concept are at Murawski, M. "Towards a More Community-Centered Museum, Part 3." *Art Museum Teaching*, Oct. 1, 2018. https://artmuseumteaching.com/2018/10/01/towards-a-more-community-centered-museum-part-3-defining-valuing-community/. Accessed 15 Nov. 2018.

# Appendix

*A Poem for Community*

No one writes poetry about the inside of a building,
Microchips don't inspire arias.
Garish fluorescence and rusty gears can't give us glimpses of the divine,
Or inspire passion and desire like the fecund whiffs of spring born of buds and flowering trees.

Enter resources. Raw materials. The fuel of industry and progress—a future of leisure bestowed by the toil of our forebears.
Step quietly. Speak humbly. Embrace communion of friends and family,
Enter a life aspirational.

# Index

For Product Safety Concerns and Information please contact our EU representative GPSR@taylorandfrancis.com
Taylor & Francis Verlag GmbH, Kaufingerstraße 24, 80331 München, Germany

www.ingramcontent.com/pod-product-compliance
Lightning Source LLC
LaVergne TN
LVHW010940110826
845149LV00013B/2688

* 9 7 8 1 0 3 2 0 8 6 7 8 1 *